Descartes Reinvented

In this study, Tom Sorell seeks to rehabilitate views that are often instantly dismissed in analytic philosophy. His book serves as a reinterpretation of Cartesianism and responds directly to the dislike of Descartes in contemporary philosophy. To identify what is defensible in Cartesianism, Sorell starts with a picture of unreconstructed Cartesianism, which is characterized as realistic, antisceptical but respectful of scepticism, rationalist, centered on the first person, dualist, and dubious of the comprehensiveness of natural science and its supposed independence of metaphysics. Bridging the gap between history of philosophy and analytic philosophy, Sorell also shows for the first time how some contemporary analytic philosophy is deeply Cartesian, despite its outward hostility to Cartesianism.

Tom Sorell is Professor of Philosophy at the University of Essex. He is the author of six books, including *Descartes* (1987), *Scientism* (1991), and *Moral Theory and Anomaly* (2000).

Descartes Reinvented

TOM SORELL

University of Essex

CAMBRIDGE
UNIVERSITY PRESS

CAMBRIDGE UNIVERSITY PRESS

Cambridge, New York, Melbourne, Madrid, Cape Town, Singapore, São Paulo

Cambridge University Press
40 West 20th Street, New York, NY 10011-4211, USA

www.cambridge.org
Information on this title: www.cambridge.org/9780521851145

First published 2005

Printed in the United States of America

A catalog record for this publication is available from the British Library.

Library of Congress Cataloging in Publication Data

Sorell, Tom.
Descartes reinvented
Tom Sorell.
p. cm.
ISBN 0-521-85114-9 (hardback)
1. Descartes, René, 1596–1650. I. Title.
B1875.S672 2005
194–dc22   2004024990

ISBN-13 978-0-521-85114-5 hardback
ISBN-10 0-521-85114-9 hardback

For Vicent Raga

Contents

Introduction

In much of Anglo-American philosophy, 'Cartesian' is a dirty word. It is applied to a wide range of unpopular views in epistemology and the philosophy of mind, views that are loosely associated with those in the *Meditations*. I shall argue that many of these unpopular views are defensible in some form, and that they help to counteract the current excesses of naturalism on the one hand, and antirationalism on the other. Contrary to naturalism, not everything that can usefully be said about knowledge or the mind comes from investigating computers, the brain, or the causal interactions between the sense organs and matter, and bad things happen when philosophy is reduced to a form of popular science. Philosophy ought of course to be informed by science, but some of its problems about mind and knowledge do not go away when scientific advances are made. Innocent Cartesianism has a role in making this clear. It can sometimes consist of asserting the endurance of the old problems in the face of breezy declarations of an entirely new agenda.

Naturalism is a tendency within Anglo-American philosophy itself; the other tendency that innocent Cartesianism counteracts – antirationalism – is influential outside philosophy, at any rate Anglo-American philosophy. This tendency, too, is marked by the use of 'Cartesian' as a term of abuse. What it is applied to this time is not the supposed illusion of a system of truths independent of natural science but a certain myth-ridden philosophical anthropology. The antirationalists dislike the idea that human beings divide up cleanly into minds and bodies. They dislike the Cartesian favouritism of mind over body, the Cartesian favouritism of intellectual capacities over sensitive and emotional ones, and, as they think, the implied favouritism of male over female. In the same way, they dislike the favouritism of rational human beings over animals and the rest of nature. And they dislike the divorce of human nature from the political. These dislikes are not always well founded when inspired by Descartes's own writings, and they do not always hang together. For example, a theory that emphasises the possibilities of rational self-control in human beings, as Descartes's own theory does, is not anti-ecological and is not necessarily unsympathetic to animals. On the contrary, the possibilities of human self-control may be the only hope for environmentalists or protectors of animal welfare. Again, although we do not get from Descartes a picture of the contribution of politics to human improvement, such a picture is not ruled out, and the outlines of a Cartesian politics are neither impossible to indicate nor unattractive when they are spelled out. As for the relation between intellectual and sensitive or emotional capacities, the critics probably exaggerate the tensions between them. A Cartesian approach is rationalistic, but it does not imply that we do or should live by reason alone. On the other hand, it insists that where reason is applicable, it can come to conclusions, both practical and theoretical, that are objectively correct.

UNRECONSTRUCTED CARTESIANISM VERSUS INNOCENT CARTESIANISM

To identify what is defensible in Cartesianism, one needs to start with a picture of unreconstructed Cartesianism – Cartesianism as it is represented in Descartes himself. This picture contains six related elements. Unreconstructed Cartesianism is (i) Realistic; (ii) antisceptical but respectful of scepticism; (iii) rationalist; (iv) centred on the first person; and (v) dualistic; finally, (vi) it doubts the comprehensiveness of natural science and its supposed independence of metaphysics.

(i) Unreconstructed Cartesianism is Realistic in the sense of asserting the mind-independence of evidence and truth for a large range of subject matters. For example, perceptible things are not necessarily as the senses make them appear, and sensory evidence does not establish their existence. The movements of bodies resembling humans do not establish that those bodies are alive or that they are directed by minds. Present-tensed evidence is neither necessary nor sufficient for the occurrence of events in the past, and so on. Being Realistic in this sense, unreconstructed Cartesianism admits the possibility of scepticism. If evidence does not constitute truth, then the possession of evidence does not constitute *knowledge* of truth, and it may even be doubted whether beliefs based on the evidence are usually true. It is in the sense of allowing for the possibility of scepticism that I say unreconstructed Cartesianism is respectful of scepticism. Indeed, in Descartes, the respectfulness goes beyond allowing for the possibility of doubt: The *Meditations* is supposed to do nothing less than *induce* doubt about whole classes of proposition.

(ii) Although unreconstructed Cartesianism is respectful of scepticism, it is antisceptical: It claims to refute scepticism by identifying a basis for the indubitability of fundamental beliefs. The basis in Descartes's version of Cartesianism is the fact that the human mind has been designed by a benign creator who would not allow it to use its reason well and arrive at falsehoods. The capacities that human beings have for finding indubitable truth are rational capacities rather than sensory ones. Although the senses have their uses for helping us to survive, and though they are sources of reliable information about some of the things that are good or bad for us, this information is often divorced from a hold on the natures of things, which is where reason comes in. Respect for scepticism is often respect for the point that human beings use sensory information when they shouldn't: They use it to make judgements about the explanations of things in nature, when the most it can acquaint us with are explananda.

(iii) Cartesian rationalism is the view that we ought ideally to form scientific beliefs and reach practical decisions on the basis of good reasons alone. 'Good reasons' may include beliefs arrived at by following certain error-avoiding steps of thought, steps that usually involve thinking twice about something the senses incline us to believe. We should not be carried along by sensory appearance, and we should not be lulled into belief by conventional wisdom or habit either. Rationalism along these lines can be associated with foundationalism, the idea that there are a small number of self-evident truths in the light of which all or most other truths are evident, or from which other truths can be derived by self-evident reasoning. Cartesian rationalism extends to ethics and the conduct of life, where it asserts that detachment from the appetites is sometimes necessary for distinguishing genuine from merely apparent goods, and for identifying an order of priority among the genuine goods.

(iv) Unreconstructed Cartesianism puts many of the fundamental questions of philosophy in the first person. 'What can I be certain of?' 'Am I alone?' 'What capacities really belong to me?' The answers to some of these questions are sometimes essentially first-personal as well. For example, in Descartes's own Cartesianism the answer to 'What can I be certain of?' consists initially of two principles. The first of these – 'I am thinking; therefore I exist' – does not remain certain if 'René Descartes is thinking' is put in place of 'I am thinking', for the existence of the man Descartes and his thinking is dubitable under the sceptical hypotheses of the *Meditations*, while 'I exist' is not. Not only are some metaphysical and epistemological questions and answers essentially first-personal for Descartes; the nature of the mind in unreconstructed Cartesianism is connected with the accessibility to the first person of most or all of the mind's thoughts.

(v) It is from the perspective of the 'I' that Descartes decides provisionally that he is complete as an intellect and a will minus the capacities of imagination and sensation, and complete minus a body. The emphasis on the first-person perspective, then, facilitates Descartes's argument for substantial dualism – for his belief in the conceptual distinctness of the mental and the physical and in the reality of entirely distinct satisfiers of those concepts. It also aggravates the problems of being clear about the way interaction between mind and body works.

(vi) Finally, unreconstructed Cartesianism insists on the need for a metaphysics distinct from and more fundamental than natural science, a metaphysics with its own subject matter of immaterial things. 'Immaterial things' includes abstract objects such as the nature of the triangle, as well as minds and the concepts required to reach conclusions in the distinct natural sciences. Metaphysics is supposed to be necessary as a preliminary to physics, because practitioners of physics need metaphysics if they are to be certain once and for all that they are capable of reaching stable general conclusions about matter at all. First philosophy provides the assurance that other sorts of philosophy or science are possible for human beings, and it is its standard of certainty that is supposed to be met in some of the sciences.

The organising thesis of unreconstructed Cartesianism is that there is an order in nature that human beings are able to capture in science, and that the makings of this science are accessible to the consciousness of every rational self. This thesis, itself expressed in terms of the self, makes the emphasis on the first person in the rest of unreconstructed Cartesianism unsurprising. Similarly for the emphasis on starting points or foundations for science. Similarly for realism, because the order of nature is what it is independently of us. The organising thesis of unreconstructed Cartesianism can also be understood as the assertion of an antisceptical position, and its explanation of how science is possible is that reason is objectively reliable.

Innocent Cartesianism is the reinterpretation, and sometimes the outright revision, of unreconstructed Cartesianism so as to meet some of the scruples of twentieth- and twenty-first-century philosophy. In other words, innocent Cartesianism sometimes results from admitting that elements of unreconstructed Cartesianism are false or not worth defending. Elements of unreconstructed Cartesianism can be rejected, however, without a repudiation of all of unreconstructed Cartesianism. On the contrary, the results of revision or reinterpretation in what follows do not take one so far from unreconstructed Cartesianism as to make the original unrecognisable. At the same time, the results of revision or reinterpretation bring one surprisingly close to some specimens of recent analytic philosophy. Surprisingly close, given the fact that producers of these specimens would sometimes disavow or express surprise at any Cartesian tendencies in their own work. Examples of innocent Cartesianism are already present in analytic epistemology and the philosophy of mind, and many of them seem to me to be philosophically sound. Though they sometimes appear to reinvent Descartes, they are seldom intended to do so. Some of the reinvention seems to be unwitting. As for the few analytic philosophers who refer approvingly to Descartes in one connection or another, they tend to lack a sense of a general Cartesian position that might be viable. At times I will call attention to what I take to be innocent Cartesianism in the recent literature, and at times I will add to it, indicating ways in which this literature is not thoroughgoing enough. Elsewhere (Chapters 1, 5, and 6), I claim that elements of unreconstructed Cartesianism themselves are reasonably innocent, understood in ways I suggest. At the end, I try to present an overview of an innocent Cartesianism in matters of theoretical and practical reason in general.

Innocent Cartesianism preserves the realism and respect for scepticism of unreconstructed Cartesianism. In particular, the coherence of sweeping Cartesian sceptical hypotheses is reasserted. On the other hand, the idea that scepticism is entirely refutable is questioned. Innocent Cartesianism also insists on the ineliminably first-person character of some epistemological questions, and some questions in the philosophy of mind. Purely externalist analyses of knowledge miss something important about the nature of epistemology, according to innocent Cartesianism, and purely subpersonal and third-personal accounts of mental states are incomplete as well. In particular, eliminativist materialist accounts and functionalist accounts leave out the subjectivity of the mental. To the extent that materialist treatments in particular are incomplete, some version of dualism is true, or acceptable pending the development of a neutral monism. No doubt the temporarily acceptable form of dualism will not be a dualism of mental and physical substances, as in Descartes, but some form of the idea that the concepts of the mental and physical mark a real difference is going to be part of what is maintained.

Innocent Cartesianism preserves rationalism, but without gearing that rationalism to God's existence and nature, and without generating a scepticism-proof argument that natural science is possible. The foundationalism of innocent Cartesianism is not a theoretically necessary response to scepticism about science but, in part, a kind of antidote to a social constructionist account of scientific truth. According to innocent Cartesianism, it is no accident that at any rate natural science is successful, and the explanation of the success consists partly in the fit between theoretical concepts and an independent world, partly in the existence of concepts playing a role similar to that which Descartes assigned to the mechanical 'simples' in physical explanation. The belief in the possibility of fit between fundamental concepts and an independent world is foundational in innocent Cartesianism, but a metaphysical proof that ideas of the 'simple material natures' are sufficient for a complete and successful science is done away with.

Instead of a proof that natural science *can* be successful, innocent Cartesianism indicates an explanation of why natural science *is* successful. This explanation is partly to do with the human ability to get beyond a sense-based understanding of phenomena and to arrive specifically at mathematical concepts that the behaviour of physical objects fits. A related ability to get beyond an appetite-based understanding of what is valuable and harmful explains our ability to perfect ourselves using practical reason. This is the ability that is central to an unreconstructed Cartesian ethics, and it is here that unreconstructed Cartesianism contributes directly to innocent Cartesianism.

The organising thesis of innocent Cartesianism is that natural science, while capable of objective truth within its domain, is not a theory of everything. There are more forms of systematic and objectively correct self-understanding and reasoning than are provided by natural science. Brain science does not tell us everything about the mind; Darwinism does not tell us everything about the place of human beings in nature and what motivates them. There are further authoritative forms of understanding, including those belonging to ethics, philosophy, and mathematics. The point of insisting on the autonomy of these forms of understanding is not to meet the supposed need for an Archimedean point from which science can be shown to be a viable enterprise, as in unreconstructed Cartesianism. It is rather to insist on the intelligibility and value of questions and answers to problems about knowledge, mind, and what human beings ought to do that cannot be pressed into a scientific mould except by force. Nevertheless, to say that natural science is not a theory of everything is not to say that natural science tells us nothing, still less that its pretensions to truth and objectivity are empty or that they mask a brute power-hunger. In the face of claims like those, innocent Cartesianism takes the side of science, truth, and objectivity just as much as unreconstructed Cartesianism does.

Innocent Cartesianism is extracted from unreconstructed Cartesianism chapter by chapter in what follows. At the beginning of the book, I argue for the intelligibility and coherence of radical scepticism and deny that the radical scepticism of Meditation One entails solipsism. Instead of a self that is entirely self-subsistent, methodological scepticism presupposes a self that is able to get outside sense-experience and able even to question the objectivity of concepts for immaterial things, including mathematical objects and the idea of God. The idea that the sceptical hypotheses of unreconstructed Cartesianism entail solipsism and are therefore inconsistent with meaningful utterance and with cogent self-reference is rejected. In Chapter 2, I turn to the Cartesian insistence that certain questions about knowledge and belief are irreducibly first-person questions, requiring answers from the perspective of consciousness. This, too, is endorsed in the course of a partial defence of what is now called 'internalism' in analytic epistemology. Chapter 3 is a defence of forms of foundationalism required to make intelligible the success of natural science. Foundationalism in these forms counts against facile relativism and the belief that explanatory concepts in the natural sciences are social constructions with no objectivity not conferred on them by a scientific community.

Chapters 4, 5, and 6 consider the Cartesian philosophy of mind and a Cartesian philosophical anthropology. In Chapter 4, arguments for the irreducibility of consciousness are reviewed and defended, but the commonly advanced claim that these arguments can be reconciled with naturalism is questioned. An innocent Cartesianism is significantly but controversially *anti*-naturalistic about the mind, just as it is uncontroversially antinaturalistic about pure mathematics and logic. The irreducibility of consciousness is consistent with a theory of the mind that does not rule out, but does not assume either, some sort of account of *how* the brain can be a personal subject of consciousness. On the other hand, an innocent Cartesianism is not consistent with some subpersonal approaches to the mind–brain relation. Chapter 5 considers the connections between Cartesian rationalism and Cartesian dualism, especially where these lead to controversial theses about the emotions. Chapter 5 also defends the view of practical reason implicit in Descartes's rationalism. Chapter 6 discusses the allegedly unacceptable consequences of Descartes's dualism and rationalism for his anthropology. Feminists complain that despite a superficial egalitarianism, Descartes is committed to saying that what is best about humans can be realised only by males. He is also supposed to be guilty of a 'masculinization of nature' and a distorted theory of the relation of the human to the rest of the animal and natural world. I argue that unreconstructed Cartesianism is much more innocent in this area than it is given credit for. Innocent Cartesianism does not *always* require significant departures from its source.

INNOCENT CARTESIANISM AND PRE-PHILOSOPHICAL WAYS OF THINKING

Although Cartesianism as it is discussed in this book is a tendency in academic philosophy, the case for the innocence of some Cartesian theses cannot entirely be separated from the fact that some ideas that started out in Descartes's writings are highly absorbed in intellectual life in the West, highly absorbed even by critics of Descartes. We might think of some of what has been absorbed as a watered-down 'Cartesian rationalism'. Rationalism in this form says that, ideally, we should hold beliefs and perform actions only on the basis of reasons we can consciously recognise as good. It implies that, ideally, we should not form beliefs or perform actions precipitately, unthinkingly, or as a matter of reflex, leaving conscious reasons out of play altogether. It also implies that if reasons for a belief do not seem compelling when brought to mind, the belief should be abandoned. Mild Cartesian rationalism – the kind that I am suggesting is second nature to us – is supported by something we might call 'Cartesian autonomy': Ideally, we ought to think for ourselves and act in our own right, and doing so means using well what freedom we have to accept or not accept propositions and carry out or not carry out our intentions. (I discuss some of these matters in Chapters 2 [acceptance of propositions] and 5 [carrying out our intentions].) The connection between Cartesian rationalism and Cartesian autonomy may be expressed by saying that when we fail to act or believe for good reasons, we fail to believe or act in our own right. It is by way of the reasons we have for beliefs and actions when we believe and act rationally that we make them ours.

Now my claim about these precepts is not just that they are Cartesian but also that they are, or have a lot in common with, things we find
truistic. By 'we' I mean not only philosophers, but educated people in
the West at the beginning of the twenty-first century. Formulations not
very different from the ones I have just given would look like commonplaces in the wider intellectual world. Thus, it seems truistic to say that
we ought to think for ourselves; that we shouldn't believe everything
is as it appears; that we shouldn't accept assertions uncritically; that
we shouldn't act in the ways we do just because it is the fashion or just
because we are required to do so by those in authority. In order to be
commonplaces these have to be recognised as commonplaces without
much argument or stage setting. I take it they *are* recognisable as commonplaces. How Cartesian any nonphilosopher is being in accepting
them, especially when they are stripped of any pointed references to
consciousness, is another question and, I concede, a tricky one. For
present purposes, however, I hope it will be enough to indicate why
Descartes's *application* of the precepts goes with, rather than against,
an early-twenty-first-century grain.

Descartes applies the precepts to arguments from authority – that
is, arguments for the truth of propositions based on the identity and
celebrity of the people propounding the propositions. The first precept of Descartes's so-called logic implies that propositions are not to
be accepted as true on the basis of authority; and there is a related
message in Descartes's refusal to count as philosophy or science mere
knowledge of what a figure from the philosophical past has said, without being able oneself to say why it is true. The rejection of intellectual
deference is second nature even to those who repudiate Descartes's
influence; so, too, I think is the aspiration to ground claims on evidence for their truth.

I do not deny that many claims which are *not* commonplaces are
to be found in Descartes's writings. I do not deny that one of the
favoured instances of thinking for oneself in Descartes is conducting
oneself through the metaphysical meditations, and that this seems to
many to be involved with solipsism, which is *not* a widespread intellectual tendency. To concede these things is not, however, to imperil the
claim that in matters of intellectual autonomy there is much common
ground between Descartes and ourselves, the intellectual culture beyond philosophy included. Someone who encounters the instruction

'Discuss critically' on an examination paper may find it hard to comply, but that is not because the instruction belongs to an alien way of life. Those who are criticised for unthinkingly regurgitating their teachers' views, or their parents' views, or the views of their social class may not in fact be regurgitating those views, or may not be doing so unthinkingly; but the point of criticising those who *are* doing so is surely not obscure. The widespread acceptance of the prohibition on plagiarism fits in here. So does the tendency to praise what is thought to be original or new. All of these tendencies are as fundamental to the Cartesian outlook as claims concerning the methodology of belief, doubt, consciousness, and God.

It may look less easy to find common ground with Cartesian rationalism in relation to action than in relation to belief. For Cartesian rationalism seems to require agents to be highly reflective rather than spontaneous, and when Descartes asks for actions to be backed by reasons, he often means reasons as *opposed* to passions or emotions or sensations. Because it is plausible to say that many actions can be worse for being consciously thought out, and because Descartes sometimes urged the suppression of emotions even in cases where to feel the emotions would attest to one's humanity or loyalty or something else with undoubted value, one can dissent perfectly reasonably from Descartes's requirements for agents. That does not mean, however, that no common ground exists between Cartesian rationalism and a modern sensibility about action. When Descartes urges the suppression of emotional behaviour, he does so partly because he connects the emotional with compulsive behaviour (see Chapter 5) and partly because he thinks that emotions can represent as good things that harm, or at any rate don't improve, the mind and the body. We can share Descartes's dislike of compulsive behaviour without supposing that all passionate behaviour is compulsive. What is more, we can agree that bodily and mental health are important goods, that emotions can sometimes point us away from these goods, and that when they do, the emotions may need to be overridden. We can also agree with the deeply Cartesian thoughts that detaching ourselves from the emotions for the purpose of controlling them is possible and sometimes useful, and that health is a matter of pursuing both goods of mind and goods of body, sometimes by strategies of self-control.

BETWEEN HISTORY OF PHILOSOPHY AND
ANALYTIC PHILOSOPHY

This book does not belong to the genre *history of philosophy*. It does not set out to teach casual critics of Cartesianism in mainstream philosophy that Descartes did not say what they think he did. It does not try to describe the intellectual climate in which what Descartes really did say would have made sense to say. Instead, it tries to find common ground between what Descartes did say and have reasons for saying, and things that are worth arguing for in philosophy as we now have it. So it lies somewhere between studies of Descartes's writings and their context and current work in philosophy of mind, metaphysics and epistemology. I hope the book will also serve as a bridge between these two bodies of work.

   The vilified Descartes of twentieth- and twenty-first-century philosophy is not the same as the canonical Descartes – the Descartes who has to be read by students of philosophy if they are to understand the subject in its current form; the vilified Descartes is not the same, either, as the historical Descartes – the Descartes of the best-informed Descartes specialists. But there is some difficulty in saying which the *real* Descartes is, as if the others were pure imposters. No doubt the historical Descartes comes closest to being the real Descartes; still, the other figures sometimes have legitimate philosophical roles, as does the idea of Cartesianism when extended beyond the ideas of Descartes himself or his avowed followers. To see this is to recognise some of the limitations of history of philosophy. To the extent that history of philosophy is a historical enterprise, it inclines the practitioner to enter into the preoccupations of Descartes as a seventeenth-century European scientist/metaphysician. To the extent that history of philosophy is a philosophical enterprise, it inclines the practitioner to remould Cartesian ideas so as to give them a clear location in live philosophical debates. The second inclination is more likely to produce caricature than the first; but the first can and often does have the drawback of being philosophically boring. As someone with an interest in a twenty-first-century philosophical agenda *as well* as the early modern period, I do not regard the problem of boringness as insignificant, and so I think that, within limits, caricature is tolerable for the sake of relevance.

Even where the claims of his modern detractors are poorly grounded in Descartes's text, or where they seem to be warranted only by a perverse reading, they belong to a kind of folk memory of Descartes in twentieth- and twenty-first-century philosophy that is important to understand in its own right and that usually has *something* important in common with what the historical Descartes said. Calling attention to this common ground is likely to be far more effective in prompting a serious reevaluation of Cartesianism than trying to persuade modern critics of Descartes that they are so wrong about him that they must have some other philosopher in mind. Were Descartes himself to come back from the dead and find the views associated with his name so unrecognisable that he would be moved to protest, '*Je ne suis pas cartésien!*', that would have no more force, necessarily, than a famous remark attributed by Engels to Karl Marx: 'All I know is that I am not a Marxist'. Marxism transcends Marx's writings; it extends to what is said and done by his appropriators, and sometimes to what they are interpreted as saying and doing by hostile critics who are sure that Marxism is dead. Mao's cultural revolution and Stalin's use of the gulags thus count for many people as prime examples of applied Marxism, even though Marx himself might have been horrified by them. In the same way, Cartesianism is bigger than Descartes, with a life of its own in a philosophical folk memory outside the history of philosophy, a folk memory largely created and sustained by those who are hostile to Cartesianism and who think it is a spent force. It would not take away the bad associations that 'Cartesianism' has for these people if it turned out, for example, that Descartes himself did not subscribe to exactly the simplified position called 'Cartesian dualism'. That position, with or without a clear presence in Descartes's writings, still has a role in mapping out a largely rejected philosophy of mind, just as applied Marxism in the form of the gulags, whether or not it is fair to name it after Marx, stakes out a historically important kind of failed twentieth-century politics.

ACKNOWLEDGEMENTS

I started thinking about the themes of this book in 1993, and then unexpectedly got involved in other projects. I went back to work on Cartesianism in 1998. Since then I have had some opportunities to

Descartes Reinvented

existence of particular bodies is put in doubt, and also the very idea of a body. The Demon is also supposed to make the existence of other minds uncertain. It undermines beliefs about the past, and it confines self-knowledge to the consciousness of the states of a disembodied ego from moment to moment.

A DOUBT THAT OVERREACHES ITSELF?

The enduring question raised by Meditation One is whether doubt overreaches itself when it goes this far. Does it call into question things that we *can't* doubt? Does it call into question the conditions under which we can mean things or have thoughts with any content? If so, then the doubt may call into question conditions for having doubts with a content, doubts *about* something. Doubt so sweeping would be self-defeating. My own view is that the doubt associated with the Dream and Demon hypotheses is *not* self-defeating. The hypotheses show that the causes of our beliefs do not generally guarantee their truth and that they sometimes produce falsehood, as when the cause of a belief is deception. The hypotheses do not show that our beliefs definitely *are* false, or that they probably are. Nevertheless, they may make us wonder whether we ought to believe the things that in a certain sense it comes naturally to us to believe. Once we have begun to wonder, we may begin to think that we have no good reason to retain many beliefs we actually hold. This starts us on the path to general uncertainty.

Descartes thinks that when general uncertainty is induced and prolonged methodically, it runs up against the indubitable in the form of metaphysical first principles, and that it is possible to get from there to a comprehensive science. I shall not be concerned in this chapter with the success or failure of Descartes's progress from near total doubt to the development of physics, mechanics, medicine, and morals. Instead, I shall pursue the question of whether Descartes can coherently get the progress to *start* from the doubt. In arguing that he can, I am going to try to separate out two conceptions of the self and the circumstances of the doubt that Descartes might be thought to rely on. One conception is that of a solipsistic subject and solipsistic conditions for doubt. Many think that Cartesian doubt overreaches itself because it lands the doubter in solipsism, and solipsism takes away the conditions under which doubts or any other thoughts can have content.

But another interpretation is possible: instead of engaging a radically isolated self, the doubt can be understood to engage a self latent in human beings that is of a kind latent in other intelligent beings. The doubt engages a species-less limited intelligence and will, something that is only incidentally realised as a human being, and whose nature can be placed on the same scale, though at a very low point on the same scale, as a being with an unlimited intelligence and will. Although neither of these conceptions belongs to an innocent Cartesianism, the second enforces a kind of cognitive humility that an innocent Cartesianism can take over. It implies that human beings have to work at being fit for science, and that this involves activating faculties that are not part of their biological endowment. I begin with this second conception.

UNRECONSTRUCTED CARTESIANISM: THE TARGET OF THE DOUBT

Biology – species membership – interferes with systematic knowledge of causes in nature: this is a large part of Descartes's message in the First and Second Meditations. According to this piece of unreconstructed Cartesianism, it is natural for human beings to rely overly on sensory information in forming conceptions of the natures of material things, as well as conceptions of everything else. Forming conceptions with the aid of the senses, Descartes claims, interferes with the discovery of general physical truths. It also interferes with the acquisition and development of mathematical thought, and with self-knowledge and the recognition of the properties of God. Descartes produces this criticism of our biological nature – in his terms, our embodiment – more than once, though sometimes indirectly. He frequently says that the ideas produced by the senses do not necessarily, and frequently do not at all, resemble the things that cause them (cf. e.g. AT VIIA 5–6; CSM I 193–4; AT XI, 3–6; CSM I, 81–2; AT VI, 32; CSM I 127).[1] The senses are

---

[1] Here and subsequently, references are by volume and page number of the standard edition of Descartes's works by Charles Adam and P. Tannery (Paris: Vrin/CNRS, 1967–76) followed by references by volume and page number to *The Philosophical Writings of Descartes*, J. Cottingham, R. Stoothoff, and D. Murdoch, trans. (Cambridge: Cambridge University Press, 1985). Adam and Tannery references begin 'AT'; 'CSM' abbreviates the *The Philosophical Writings*; 'CSM III' abbreviates vol. 3 of *The Philosophical Writings*, Cottingham, Stoothoff, Murdoch, and A. Kenny, trans. (Cambridge: Cambridge University Press, 1991).

the main representatives in his theory of knowledge of human biology. All of the sensory reactions human beings have are the result of the operations of the internal parts of the body when stimulated at the sensory surfaces. In this latter respect we do not differ, except in respect of differences between the organs, from other animals (cf. AT VI 55f; CSM I 139ff). Nor do living animal bodies, our own included, differ from machines with the machine counterparts of human organs (*Treatise on Man* passim). In all animals, sensory reactions are purely mechanical: purely the effects of movements of the internal parts. Biological differences within the animal kingdom are solely a matter of differences between the bodies, their internal parts, and their movements. What sets human beings apart from and above other animals is not something biological or even natural – our walking erect, say, or our having a big brain – but something immaterial and metaphysical: the rational soul. Although this operates via the human brain in a living human being, it could exist without it. And in a certain sense it exists to counterbalance the purely mechanical imprints of the sensory system. For it is the rational soul that enables us to reflect on and consider the resemblance between sensory material and its causes, as well as the consequences of purely impulsive behaviour.

This rational soul is what, according to unreconstructed Cartesianism, enables human beings to rise above confused sensory ideas of particular bodies, conceive the nature of matter, and speculatively reconstruct its differentiation into the elements, as well as their lawlike combination into the systems of the planets, Earth, and terrestrial bodies. Or, in other words, the rational soul is the seat of scientific capacity in us. But the rational soul is not the same as the human being. The human being, as Descartes conceives it, is the union of the rational soul with the human animal. Far from being the seat of scientific capacity, the human being or embodied rational soul is the seat of prejudice, undigested sensory information, curiosity, and rash inference. The beginning of science is consciousness of the false beliefs cultivated over a lifetime of embodiment. Consciousness of false beliefs is consciousness on the part of a rational soul, but a rational soul that is mostly dormant in a standard human lifetime. Metaphysical exercises – exercises in sweeping methodical doubt – awaken the capacities and concepts in the rational soul that can correct for error, prejudice, rash inference, and the blind enquiry that curiosity prompts. These capacities and concepts are innate in the rational soul and ineradicable, but they can be overridden or hidden by the operation of the senses, which, according to Descartes, are designed not for discovering the natures of things but for pursuing and avoiding what will benefit or harm the individual living body. Sensible qualities are guides to whether the things that produce them are good or bad for us, but not to why they are harmful or beneficial, or to their effects on other inanimate things. Grasping the natures of things means uncovering what patterns of extension and motion they conform to, and these cannot be read off their colours, smells, felt textures, or temperatures. These patterns are accessible only to reason. But unleashing the reason in one can mean suppressing the sensory, in a way deserting one's humanity and animality.

The point of unreconstructed Cartesianism about reason, and of doubt as a means of activating reason, becomes clear by identifying the philosophical position Descartes is up against. When he says that sensory ideas do not resemble what they are ideas of; when he says that as human beings we are not naturally equipped for science but need a method of science and a capacity for doing science that is usually only dormant in us, his claims are diametrically opposed to Aristotle's. For Aristotle the human senses bring us into contact with the natures of things: The forms that indicated the essences of natural kinds are actually part of what the human senses take in, and for someone to have a sensory experience of an F is for the sensory experience to have F in it, which the human mind subsequently abstracts. On this theory the resemblance between a human sensory idea and what it is an idea of is a condition of sense-perception itself. The mind does not transform or correct sensory content. Instead, it allows properties common to observed things to register in the mind as a by-product of repeated presentation to the senses. The idea of systematic sense-based error in human beings is foreign to Aristotelian epistemology, and the explanatory forms cited by Aristotelian demonstrations of observed effects are always properties of things open to unaided human observation. There is no equation in the Aristotelian philosophy of science of the explanatory with the microstructural or with what things are made of. On the contrary, explanatory principles are always close to the observational surface. In a sense the natures of things and human observation are made for each other.

The recognised 'sciences' at the time Descartes was writing were Aristotelian. The philosophy of science that prevailed was also Aristotelian. According to the Aristotelian philosophy of science, an explanation is a syllogism in which an observed fact of the form S is P is shown to be necessary by premises of the form S is M and M is P, where M is a 'middle term' showing a connection between S and P, and the premises of the syllogism are more evident than the conclusion. Aristotelian explanations conforming to this pattern strike the modern ear as uninformative and false, or else uninformative and truistic. Why do apples fall from the boughs of trees? Because apples are terrestrial things and terrestrial things tend to move toward the centre of the Earth. Why do the stars in the sky form the patterns we identify as constellations night after night? Because stars are celestial bodies and the heavens are unchanging. In Cartesian physics 'celestial' and 'terrestrial' are not explanatory categories, and the falsehood that the heavens are unchanging, far from being an explanandum in physics, is one of the prejudices Descartes thinks his mind was cluttered with by Aristotelian teachings.

Aristotelian physics, especially celestial physics or astronomy, was in a sort of crisis in the early seventeenth century. Galileo and Kepler identified big anomalies and provided alternative explanations. Two of the three essays in Descartes's *Discourse and Essays* were an attempt to provide un-Aristotelian explanations of selected optical and meterological phenomena, and the *Discourse* presented a veiled anti-Aristotelian philosophy of science. Its ultimate explanatory concepts were extension, motion, shape, and position, rather than, as in Aristotle, the qualities of heat and cold, wet and dry. Reason rather than sense is the main cognitive capacity underlying science. Metaphysical doubt, rather than sense, elicits the use of reason and the discovery first of the principal metaphysical truths and then the general truths of physics, biology, and psychology. The *Meditations* is a sort of sequel to and enlargement on the *Discourse*, especially its Part IV. What the *Discourse* merely sketches – the method of doubt and its use to discover first the *cogito* and then the proof of a nondeceiving God – the *Meditations* unfolds in detail, and in such a way as to allow the reader to enter. But the broad purposes of the *Essays* are still in force in Meditation One. Descartes hopes to undo the influence of Aristotle, only by exposing all sense-based science as doubtful, rather than by presenting his own un-Aristotelian solutions to selected problems of physics.

In the *Discourse* and *Essays* Descartes conducts his anti-Aristotelian campaign by reviewing the scientific subjects he was taught by his Aristotelian schoolmasters. In the *Meditations* the upshot of doubt for scientific subjects is not so close to the surface. But it is not entirely suppressed. When Descartes wonders what general conclusion is to be drawn from the hypothesis that all conscious experience might be a dream, he first infers that not all dream content is necessarily unreal, that some content – simple and universal content – has got to be real for dreams to be about anything. This simple and universal content includes number, shape, place, time, and so on. All the dream threatens, Descartes says, is the reality of content compounded in the wrong way out of these simples. And this includes the content of some of the (Aristotelian) sciences:

... physics, astronomy, medicine, and all other disciplines which depend on the study of composite things, are doubtful, while arithmetic, geometry, and other subjects of this kind, which deal only with the simplest and most general things, regardless of whether they exist in nature or not, contain something certain or indubitable. (AT VII 20; CSM II 14)

So the Dream counts against most of the traditional sciences. And even arithmetic and geometry cannot retain their certainty when considered together with facts about the creation and manipulability of the human mind. The simples that apparently *have* to exist might not have existed, if God had decided not to create them. And he might have decided not to create them while deciding to make it seem to us as if they had to. Or, if *God* wouldn't have arranged things this way, perhaps a sufficiently powerful demon could have. Descartes does not dwell on the dubitability of the simples, or the sciences of the simple. And belief in their existence is only very briefly suspended. But by the end of the First Meditation all of the sciences are discredited, and of these the most doubtful are the Aristotelian ones.

In Meditation Two Descartes goes on to attack the Aristotelian philosophy of science. He imagines himself devoid of a body and senses and yet still in existence. That is, he imagines himself in existence and yet not a man or human being. (This is to imagine the impossible according to Aristotle, for each of us is, according to Aristotle, essentially human.) In this sense-less and species-less state, in the absence of an external world, he finds in himself the ingredients of metaphysics and physics. He finds in himself the idea of himself, the general idea of a thinking thing or *res cogitans*, the idea of God, the idea of extension, the idea of motion and so on – the very ideas that he thinks suffice for the speculative reconstruction of the operations of the planetary system, the existence of the Earth, and the variety and operations of bodies on Earth. In short, he sketches a physics that is wholly un-Aristotelian and a philosophy of science that in its fundamentals – in its conception of matter and laws of motion – is wholly rationalist, and therefore wholly un-Aristotelian as well.[2]

The idea that a rational, species-less self is the residue of the doubt is less familiar in twentieth-century criticism of Descartes than the idea that a sort of solipsistic self results from the reflection of Meditation One, and I return to this latter idea in the section after next. But the idea of a species-less self is also considered suspect in current philosophy, especially when the species-less self is supposed to belong to a class of thinking things that also contains God. The more human beings free their thought from the influences of the senses, the more human thought is supposed by Descartes to approximate to divine thought. But the comparison with God invites many kinds of philosophical illusion, according to some philosophers, and is probably no more innocent an element of Cartesianism than solipsism is.

THE SPECIES-LESS SELF AND GOD

In Descartes, as in traditional theology, God is supposed to have not only a nonsensory knowledge of reality but an *ideal* knowledge of reality. Ideal knowledge means, among other things, comprehensive knowledge. God is omniscient. All truths, or perhaps only all general truths, are known to God. Omniscience is tied to God's role as the creator of reality; his knowledge is foreknowledge. There is no question of his finding *out* how things are, as human beings have to. He determines how they are. This determination is strict. There are no slips between cup and lip; for God to decide that things will be thus and so is logically sufficient for their being thus and so. This determination of reality by God's will extends to mathematical reality,

---

[2] The qualification 'in its fundamentals' is important because Descartes thinks that derivative parts of physics – the applications of general principles to particular phenomena – do require the senses. He is no believer in a totally a priori physics.

according to Descartes. He distinctively maintains that God's concurrence is required even to make 2 and 2 add up to 4. Human beings are in an entirely different case. Very little of what is real or true is brought about or made by human beings, and there can be thoughts in human minds that are false, and ideas with no resemblance to an external world. Even where things they intend are within their power, things can go wrong for human beings, because, unlike God, they are in control of only some of the conditions of the outcomes they intend. In short, impotence and fallibility are facts of human life that keep human beings very far from the ideal.

God is also a spiritual being. He is not embodied, and he has no sense-organs. Because he also has a comprehensive knowledge of reality, reality is not made to be known by sense-organs, still less human sense-organs. Perhaps knowledge by means of the sense-organs is possible, but there can be no knowledge that is irreducibly sensory; otherwise God would lack it. Instead, whatever there is sensory knowledge of must be knowable by God's knowing faculty. This knowing faculty is pure intellect. Human beings cannot possibly have the same intellect as God has, according to unreconstructed Cartesianism, for God's is infinite and ours is discoverably limited. Still, we can enjoy nonsensory knowledge of some things – for example, the axioms and theorems of geometry, some truths of arithmetic, and some of the metaphysical truths. Our nonsensory knowledge of these things may be hard-won and incomplete and have many other shortcomings, therefore making it quite different from God's, but it is arguably knowledge we have no thanks to the human senses. It is arguably knowledge we could have in common with other creatures with different sensory capacities. Although it is probably a poor kind of nonsensory knowledge by comparison with God's, it is of a kind the ideal of which is marked by God's nonsensory knowledge. In a sense, God and human beings can enjoy the same type of knowledge. In a more robust sense, according to Descartes, they can also enjoy the same type of will. For although God's will rules throughout reality, each human will is supposed to be able to rule all powerfully within each self (Med. IV, AT VII 57–8; CSM I 40). It is against this background that Descartes says that God and the human intellect-and-will both belong to the same kind: the kind *res cogitans*.

The correct understanding of what human beings and God have in common is supposed to be possible once the mind has discerned a self that survives the destruction in the imagination of the body and senses – that is, a self that survives the conditions of the Demon hypothesis. This is a self understood quite abstractly as a subject of thought, or a subject of capacities of judgement and will, and not as someone located in a particular room in France with certain memories, current sensations and experiences, inclinations or plans. Is the self understood in that way understood *too* abstractly? And when God, understood in Descartes's way, sets the pattern for what subjects of thought are like, is there any room left for recognisably *human* subjects of thought?

To take the second question first, much depends on what it means to say that God 'sets the pattern' for subjects of thought. If it is a requirement for being a subject of thought that the subject be God-like in the sense of having very considerable cognitive capacities, then Descartes's approach seems unattractive. But, as already indicated, this is not the way in which God sets the pattern for counting as *res cogitans*. '[I]f I examine the faculties of memory and imagination, or any others,' Descartes says, 'I discover that in my case each of these faculties is weak and limited, while in the case of God it is immeasurable' (AT VII 57; CSM II 40). My faculties are of the same kind as God's even if they are unspeakably weak and limited in comparison with his. In other words, I can be very *un*God-like as *res cogitans* – at least when it comes to cognitive capacities – and still have capacities in common with God that make us belong to the same kind. It is true that when it comes to the will, I am supposed to be *more* God-like. But this is because of a deflationary conception of what the will is for. 'It is both extremely ample and also perfect of its kind' (AT VII 58; CSM 40). It is extremely ample when its whole job is to affirm or deny or pursue or avoid without the feeling of external compulsion (AT VII 57–8). So long as it does not make judgements as a matter of reflex or make itself a vehicle for inclinations, the will does all it should. The exercise of the divine will, on the other hand, is on nothing less than a cosmic scale: It cements together what are otherwise independent individual moments of each thing's existence (cf AT VII 49; CSM II 33).

Does the comparison with God exaggerate the human capacity for nonsensory thought? Does it exaggerate our capacity for nonsensory thoughts of external things and ourselves? Bernard Williams has found in Descartes a commitment to the intelligibility of what he calls 'an absolute conception' and a commitment to the accessibility of this conception through 'pure enquiry'.[3] The absolute conception is the one we might use to identify, in particular, experiences or thoughts of an independent reality, those aspects that were contributed by their being *our* experiences or thoughts. The absolute conception would thus enable us to identify what was contributed to our representations by living at a certain time and place, by belonging to a community with a certain tradition, by having a certain individual physical makeup, by having a human constitution. Whatever was left over, when these elements were set aside, would be the contribution of that independent reality itself – varieties of extension and motion and a few immaterial entities in Descartes's version of the absolute conception. The absolute conception is problematic, however, because if it can be ours, it, too, must have some parochial elements. On the one hand, its pretensions to absoluteness are compromised by its being someone's or some species' conception; on the other hand, absoluteness is what science or systematic knowledge seems to aim at.[4]

Did Descartes think that human conceptions of immaterial and material things were capable of a kind of refinement that would remove any trace of their having been thought up by anyone, so that they could pass for pure facts? I am aware of no reason to think so. The elements of any would-be absolute conception are what Descartes calls 'simple and universal things', but these are simple and universal relative to a finite mind[5] and not necessarily relative to God's. A finite mind is not necessarily a finite *human* mind, and apparently there are other finite minds 'incomparably more perfect' than ours but inferior to God's – the minds of angels, for example (AT V 56; CSM III 322). But 'simplicity' is a mind-relative notion. In Descartes's writings it is usually defined as what can be understood on its own, or what cannot be understood better by reference to something else

---

[3] Bernard Williams, *Descartes: The Project of Pure Enquiry* (Harmondsworth: Penguin, 1978), pp. 64f.

[4] For further reflections on what makes the absolute conception problematic, see Hilary Putnam, 'Bernard Williams and the Absolute Conception of the World' in *Renewing Philosophy* (Cambridge, Mass.: Harvard University Press, 1992), pp. 80–107.

[5] 'Simple with respect to our intellect', as it is put in the early *Regulae* (AT X 418, 419; CSM I 44).

than on its own. But how well something is understood is explained in Descartes by reference to the kind of impact it makes on an attentive mind, not on its being a component of a fact impersonally understood.

It is true that the simple is relative to an attentive mind that is detached from the senses, but is there some pretension to transcend all representation or to achieve an absolute conception in the simple so conceived? Again, the answer seems to be 'No'. Although Descartes wants to get away from identifying the material with what feels solid to the touch and occupies a region of a visual field; although he thinks 'feels solid' can be illuminatingly explained in terms of the interactions between parts of the human body like the hand and the surface and composition of, for example, a tree branch, the preferred mechanical explanation is not supposed to draw on concepts that are absolutely basic. The mechanical explanation shows how a certain stimulation of the hand in a normal living body could produce a sensation of solidity. It does not purport to tell us how God did or must have made living bodies or tree branches to produce a sensation of solidity. A Cartesian explanation, even one meeting the standards of certainty of Descartes's *Discourse*, purports only to be coherent and simple and to lead to a simulation of the phenomena (To Mersenne 27 May 1638, AT II 141–2; CSM III 103). A God's eye view, which does have a claim to being absolute, is probably closed off to us.

Descartes's conception of the tree branch and its solidity aspires to detachment but not absoluteness. It conforms quite closely to what Thomas Nagel calls the 'physical conception of objectivity', which

is not the same thing as our idea of what physical reality is actually like, but [which] has developed as part of our method of arriving at a truer understanding of the physical world, a world that is presented to us initially but somewhat inaccurately through sensory perception.

The development goes in stages, each of which gives a more objective picture than the one before. The first step is to see that our perceptions are caused by the action of things on us, through their effects on our bodies, which are themselves parts of the physical world. The next step is to realize that since the same physical properties that cause perceptions in us through our bodies also produce different effects on other physical things and can exist without causing any perceptions at all, their true nature must be detachable from their perceptual appearance and need not resemble it. The third step is to try to form a conception of that true nature independent of its appearance either to us or other types of perceivers. This means not only not thinking of the physical world from our particular point of view, but not thinking of it from a more general human perceptual point of view either: not looking how it looks, feels, smells, tastes, or sounds. These secondary qualities then drop out of our picture of the external world, and the underlying primary qualities such as shape, size, weight, and motion are thought of structurally.[6]

Descartes certainly thought that the primary quality conception could be shared by human beings and by creatures that had no sensory capacities. If 'an angel were in a human body, he would not have sensations as we do, but would simply perceive the motions which are caused by external objects' (To Regius, January 1642; AT III 493; CSM III 206). These are the motions we can conceive or understand – rather than perceive – with Descartes's mechanical theory of sense. But he never claims that, when we conceive the motions as the theory tells us to, we are rising to God's conception.

Just as it is only a *more* objective conception – not a perfectly objective conception – that Descartes's physics is supposed to give us of external bodies, so it is a more objective conception – not necessarily a perfectly objective conception – that Descartes's metaphysics is supposed to give us of the human mind. The more objective conception of the human mind is the conception of it by way of those faculties that human beings can share with God and the angels or 'intelligent creatures in the stars or elsewhere' (To Chanut, 6 June 1647, AT V 55; CSM III 321). Or, more strictly, it is that minimum set of faculties which we can credit ourselves with and still conceive of ourselves as being the *same* things. I could lose my memory and my sensory capacities and yet still conceive of myself going on existing, but I could not do that with less than a faculty of the understanding and the will. Perhaps the test of subtracting faculties until one reaches a confused conception of the self will not yield a self with the same faculties as human beings could conceivably share with *any* intelligence, no matter how it was realised biologically. But Descartes seems to be correct in holding, what is second nature to hold even in anti-Cartesian philosophy today, that to have a mind is not necessarily to take the form of a terrestrial creature, or even a biologically realised creature.

We are now in a position to revive the question that was left hanging earlier: Is the conception of a *res cogitans* too austere or abstract to give

---

[6] *The View from Nowhere* (Oxford: Oxford University Press, 1986), p. 14.

us a conception of a self? This is a different question from whether having a mind and being a *res cogitans* are the same thing. But in Meditation Two the thought that Descartes finds accessible when he finds that 'I am a rational animal' is doubtful, or when 'I am a human being' is doubtful, is 'I am a thinking thing'. There is a certain tension between conceiving oneself as a self and conceiving oneself as a pure intellect. For to be a self is to have a perspective in which a particular spatial location is presented as here, and a certain time is presented as now. The pure intellect communes with eternal truths and simple and universal things. Not here, not *this* place, but place in general. Not now, not *this* time, but time in general. Or as Descartes puts it in *The Principles* (Pt. I, 48), '*substance, duration, order, number*' that are common to all classes of things, the two ultimate classes themselves – the mental (defined by the attribute of thought), the physical (defined by the attribute of extension), and the types of things that arise from the union of the mental and physical – sensation, emotion, and appetite. These types of things do not present themselves to a self – as opposed to a mind – and a pure intellect would register thought or a type of thought where a self would register a particular thought going on now in me. The doubting self engages the pure intellect not in having a particular thought – having an experience as of being seated by a fire – but in detaching itself from all such thoughts and seeing the common property of their all being objects of immediate awareness, that is of their being thought. Descartes slurs over this difference between the doubting self and the pure intellect in the doubting self. He cannot identify the two and confine the objects of the pure intellect, as he seems to wish to do, to general things. But this in no way discredits Descartes's idea that a more objective conception of the self or the mind than the native one would abstract away what is contributed by a particular species. Nor does it discredit Descartes's idea that the detachment brought about by the method of doubt makes the species-less self more accessible.

THE SOLIPSISTIC SELF AS THE RESIDUE OF THE DOUBT: THREE CLAIMS OF INCOHERENCE

The idea of a species-less self, I have been claiming, is anti-Aristotelian. Although Descartes was explicit about the anti-Aristotelian message of the *Meditations* in correspondence,[7] it was not supposed to be obvious from the text to a seventeenth-century audience, and it does not leap to the eye of the twenty-first-century reader either. The bearing of the doubt on Aristotle, in particular, has not attracted much notice outside the writings of Descartes specialists. Instead, people have been struck by supposed indications of solipsism in the method of doubt. Although Cartesian certainty eventually extends to truths about God and the soul, the deductions of mathematics, the general truths of a mechanistic physics, and a moral psychology for a social existence, it *starts out*, Descartes's twentieth- and twenty-first-century critics point out, by being radically egocentric. Until God's existence is proved, doubt is possible wherever the certainty of the ego's existence is insufficient for certainty about the existence or nature of anything else. Against this background, what is extreme about the doubt is not that it makes the scope for possible uncertainty very wide but that its limits are set initially by the limits of inner space. Everything beyond the contents of immediate experience is uncertain. The axioms of arithmetic and geometry fall outside immediate experience; so do many other things that are very hard to find grounds for questioning. The objection here is not that Descartes pursues epistemological questions in the first person, though, as we shall see in the next chapter, that, too is complained about in twentieth-century philosophy. It is that the 'I' which is engaged by the doubt seems a mere trickle of consciousness with little duration, no unity, and no location in a wider world. This 'I' is supposed to be a site for quite complicated thoughts – about its own nature, the nature and existence of bodies, and the relation of its own nature and the existence and nature of bodies to their creator: God. But it is also important to Descartes's argument that whole classes of pre-philosophical thoughts are unavailable to this shrunken 'I' – and one question is whether *any* thoughts can be available to it. Perhaps there is no thinking of or about anything and no possibility of linguistic reference to anything, either, if all the demon leaves us with is a sort of conscious vanishing point.

---

[7] '... I may tell you, between ourselves, that these six Meditations contain all the foundations of my physics. But please do not tell people, for that might make it harder for supporters of Aristotle to approve them. I hope that readers will gradually get used to my principles, and recognise their truth, before they notice that they destroy the principles of Aristotle' (to Mersenne, 28 January 1641. AT III 298; CSM III 173).

There are familiar arguments about the indispensability for thought and for linguistic reference of an external world and a linguistic community. I shall consider several such arguments and shall claim that Descartes's sceptical hypotheses do not take away the conditions for thought and talk. Some unreconstructed Cartesianism – about the self-intimation of thoughts and first-person authority about them – needs revision, but the makings of a defensible Cartesianism, especially about self-reference, remain.

In a famous article entitled 'Brains-in a-Vat',[8] Putnam tries to point out a tension between what is required for formulating a sceptical hypothesis and what the hypothesis permits if it is true. A doubt that extended to all facts, Wittgenstein says, would put into doubt the meanings of words, including the words needed to express doubt.[9] Putnam claims something similar, but on the basis of considerations about meaning that are in part foreign to Wittgenstein.

Putnam invites us to imagine that all the experiences we each seem to have are in fact the experiences of disembodied brains floating in a nutrient solution.

The nerve endings have been connected to a super-scientific computer which causes the person whose brain it is to have the illusion that everything is perfectly normal. There seem to be people, the objects, the sky etc.; but really all the person (you) is experiencing is the result of electronic impulses travelling from the computer to the nerve endings. The computer is so clever that if the person tries to raise his hand, the feedback from the computer will cause him to 'see' and 'feel' the hand being raised. Moreover, by varying the program, the evil scientist can cause the victim to 'experience' (or hallucinate) any situation or environment that the evil scientist wishes. He can also obliterate the memory of the brain operation, so that the victim will seem to himself to have always been in this environment. It can even seem to the victim that he is sitting and reading these very words about the amusing but quite absurd situation that there is an evil scientist who removes people's brains from their bodies and places them in a vat of nutrients which keep the brains alive.[10]

---

[8] In Putnam's *Reason, Truth, and History* (Cambridge: Cambridge University Press, 1981), pp. 1–21. The claim that the argument of this paper is Wittgensteinian appears on p. 20.

[9] *On Certainty*, ed. G. E. M. Anscombe and G. H. von Wright; D. Paul amd G. E. M. Anscombe, trans. (Oxford: Blackwell, 1969) §104. Subsequently referred to as 'OC' with a section number.

[10] Ibid., p. 6.

Putnam claims that, although the brains-in-a-vat hypothesis (there are actually many brains in vats in his story) is consistent with physical law, it cannot possibly be true. The reason is that the brains cannot think the thought that they might be brains in the vat. And the reason they cannot do so is that the hypothesis rules out their interacting with any brains or vats, and these interactions are necessary for reference in thought or talk to brains or vats. Otherwise reference is magic, and terms reach out inexplicably to whatever they designate.

Is the brains-in-a-vat hypothesis really self-refuting, as Putnam claims? According to him, the most that brains in his story could think of is 'brains-in-the-image' and 'vats-in-the-image';[11] so the thought that I am a brain in a vat is always false when the thinker is a brain in the vat. In that sense, the hypothesis is supposed to be self-refuting. But is it? Putnam does not say whether the brains are taken from competent speakers, or how concepts of any kind for vats or brains, even vats-in-the-image or brains-in-the-image get into the evil scientist's subjects. Suppose that before their brains were taken out, the people preyed upon by Putnam's evil scientist learned the words 'brain' and 'vat' in the normal way, through interactions with brains and vats and other embodied speakers of the language. Suppose that the brains of these people preserve the traces of that language learning. Can there *then* be thoughts of brains in vats on the part of these brains? If the answer is 'No', it cannot be on the ground that these people refer magically in thought to brains in vats. They refer no more magically than ordinary speakers whose interactions with brains and vats are intermittent or largely vicarious. On the other hand, if the once linguistically competent but disembodied brains *can* refer, then why can't the ones in Putnam's story? Is it because the relevant linguistic programmes run independently of nonverbal stimuli, in the stimuli of brains and vats? If so, how are the brains able to refer to *anything*, even brains-in-the-image and vats-in-the-image? Putnam never satisfactorily answers this question. More worryingly, it is never clear in his argument whether causal interaction with vats and brains is supposed to be necessary for references in thought to brains or vats. Some critics have even wondered whether normal reference and the

---

[11] Ibid., p. 15.

formulability of epistemological scepticism are ruled out on Putnam's own assumptions.[12]

Suppose that the evil scientist does not stoop to disembodiment. He inserts an implant into some speakers' heads, and, when he wishes to, he interrupts their normal experience of the world and substitutes for it whatever he likes. He might substitute experience that was a facsimile of what they would have had if the implant had not been activated. He might substitute experience that was radically different, and that might seem to the subjects like a sudden, extreme hallucination. These possibilities certainly feed radical epistemological scepticism, but they are entirely consistent with the ability on the part of subjects to *formulate* this scepticism. It is even a question why formulability on the part of subjects matters, if there are grounds for the hypothesis impersonally speaking. Unless the conditions for radical scepticism always exclude conditions under which a sceptical hypothesis is justified, it is unclear what weight to give to an argument like Putnam's about formulability.

I now turn to two Wittgensteinian lines of thought that question the coherence of demonic deception. According to Wittgenstein's *On Certainty*, there are sentences that appear to have ordinary truth conditions, that appear to be open to negation and to assertion, but that in fact cannot be treated as if they might be false by speakers of a language. 'Every human being has parents' is an example; so is 'The earth has existed for many years past'. Treating these sentences as if they couldn't be false is a condition of a practice of significant assertion within a region of language, according to Wittgenstein. But all of these sentences are supposed to be able to be doubtful under the hypothesis of the demon. Some are even included by Descartes among the 'prejudices' of childhood. According to Wittgenstein, they are radically misdiagnosed as prejudices and are probably beyond truth and falsehood.

A second, not altogether unconnected, Wittgensteinian line of thought is to the effect that many first-person psychological sentences have to be treated as if criteria of truth and truthfulness for them coincided. In other words, there is a convention that users of these sentences cannot be understood to be mistaken. The sentences can

---

[12] See, for example, Mark Sacks, *The World We Found* (London: Duckworth, 1989), ch. 3.

possibly be false only where, unusually, speakers use them to deceive others. According to Wittgenstein, the deceiving use of the first-person sentences is special and derivative, and not, as in the standard, nonpsychological, case, a possibility as soon as the truthful use of a sentence is. The basic use of 'I am in pain' or 'I have a headache' is as a linguistic counterpart of pre-linguistic expressions of pain, such as crying out, wincing, and grimacing. In their case, too, deception is possible, but the subject has to learn to suppress the natural link between the expression of pain and what is expressed. It is the same with the use of the sentence 'I am in pain'. It is introduced into language in connection with the natural expression of pain, and it does not lose this connection in its ordinary use. If 'I am in pain' came to be used more frequently by people who only pretended to be in pain than by people who actually were in pain, that would constitute a significant disruption of the linguistic practice associated with 'pain'. In some passages in Descartes, not just some but *all* first-person psychological sentences appear to be associated with a guarantee against mistake on the part of the user, and the basis of the guarantee is very different. The basis is that all thoughts and sensations – sensations are a special case of thoughts – immediately make themselves known in the consciousness of the subject. They are self-identifying and self-implicating. This is a world away from the Wittgensteinian diagnosis, which locates the impossibility of a mistake in a linguistic convention, itself dependent on the brute fact that in human beings certain behaviour means pain.

One element of the Cartesian theory of first-person sentences, if indeed it *is* Descartes's theory, can immediately be rejected. This is the claim that *all* psychological states are self-implicating. It seems clear that many beliefs can be unconscious, and Descartes himself at times commits himself to as much, because he appears to think that the habit of trusting to the senses makes it hard to activate the understanding and bring to consciousness the implicit acceptance of some truths available to it. Though he sometimes writes as if whatever is thought must be present to consciousness, he may actually be committed to the weaker thesis that whatever is thought must be *accessible* in principle to consciousness. This leaves room for the possibility that some thoughts are not self-implicating and self-identifying.

There remains, however, the disagreement over the nature of the immunity to error of first-person sentences about pain. Although the matter is rarely addressed specifically by Descartes, the following passage, from section 45 of Part One of *The Principles of Philosophy*, takes us some way forward:

A perception which can serve as the basis for a certain and indubitable judgement needs to be not merely clear but also distinct. I call a perception 'clear' when it is present and accessible to the attentive mind – just as we say that we see something clearly when it is present to the eye's gaze and stimulates it with a sufficient degree of strength and accessibility. I call a perception 'distinct' if, as well as being clear, it is so sharply separated from all other perceptions that it contains within itself only what is clear.

To be vividly and distinctly presented to an attentive mental gaze: That is what is required of the content of clear and distinct judgement. Pain is vivid in the required way, and the experience that corresponds to 'I am in pain' probably passes Descartes's test for clarity *and* distinctness. (Other thoughts, those that locate pain in a limb, contain elements that are not clear; so not *every* first-person thought about pain – 'The pain in my hand has gotten worse' – describes something clearly and distinctly perceived.)

Being in the foreground of the visual field of the mind's eye makes what is seen there unmistakeable, according to Descartes's metaphor for clarity. Going by what the metaphor suggests, the sentence 'I am in pain' is immune to error because the pain imposes itself on the mind's eye just as it is, and all the elements referred to in the sentence are co-present with the mental or verbal utterance of it. On this model, people who are at one remove from someone in pain have no impact made on their mind's eye, and that is why they can make mistakes about others and why they have to rely on those whose mind's eye *is* affected. This is clearly a more suspect way than Wittgenstein's of explaining the fact that we don't typically correct or doubt people who say that they are in pain. For one thing, it makes it mysterious that third persons are responsible for teaching first persons to refer to their own pains. The Wittgensteinian account makes this fact unmysterious: It is the connection between pain and its pre-linguistic expression that allows first-person reference to pain to be made. Again, if 'I am in pain' reaches out to a self and to an element only that self is aware of, as the Cartesian construal seems to suggest, it is legitimate to press questions about the correct *identification* of the self and its mental contents, questions that when pressed are unanswerable, just as Wittgenstein's private language argument claims.

But the Wittgensteinian account is also questionable. It seems to suggest that first-person sentences about pain do not contain *references* to the self or to pain at all and do not have meanings that are a function of the meanings of their parts. In that case, how are we to coordinate first-person sentences about pain with sentences in which self-reference does seem to succeed, as in 'I feel faint' or in which there seems to be genuine reference to pain, as in 'My headache today has lasted longer than the one I had yesterday'? Again, how are first-person sentences about pain to be related to other first-person sentences in which 'I' refers and the meaning of the whole does seem to be a function of the meaning of the parts, as in 'I am taller than my daughter'?

I shall claim that self-reference is difficult for any theory to make sense of, and that some uses of 'I' seem to drive us back to the Cartesian model, in which the self-implicatingness, though not the alleged self-identifyingness, of conscious states is important. These uses of 'I' include those identified by Wittgenstein in *The Blue Book* as 'uses of "I" as subject'. These are not necessarily central uses of 'I', but nor do they seem to be uses that we can ignore in an adequate account of self-reference. These uses do not reveal the 'real' or metaphysically most important reference of 'I', but they are not convincingly discounted either as philosophically inspired misuses of 'I'. They leave a Cartesian residue in the theory of self-reference. After discussing these uses, I return to the question of whether Cartesian certainty is primarily certainty about things in inner space. I shall claim that while Cartesian certainty is always connected to the conscious effect of a thought, the subject matter of that thought is hardly ever psychological, and the conscious effect of the thought is not sufficient for truth. What is crucial for truth is the connection between the conscious effect and the constitution of the mind in which the effect occurs.

INNOCENT CARTESIANISM IN THE THEORY OF SELF-REFERENCE

Descartes certainly thinks that *self*-reference is possible when the Demon hypothesis has driven the 'I' into its own experiences in the present. He not only thinks that 'I' and 'me' continue to refer; he thinks they pick out what he claims is the true self – an immaterial thinking thing or soul, as opposed to a living human being. This view about what 'I' really refers to is highly disputable. Could it turn out that many perfectly standard-looking uses of 'I' – as in 'I have gained two pounds' or 'I can't get into these trousers' – are somehow secondary or derivative, notwithstanding the fact that they are probably even more central to our repertoire with the first-person pronoun than 'I am thinking' or 'I am in pain'? And the derivativeness apart, could it really turn out to be *profoundly* true that I can't get into my trousers, because no referent of 'I' is spatial, and so no referent of 'I' is a *possible* candidate for containment in trousers? The appropriateness of these questions is perhaps a sign that the first-person perspective required by the doubt is not capturable by a first-person pronoun whose use we understand. Then there are all the thoughts – for example, 'I have no senses'; 'Body, shape, extension, movement, and place are mere chimeras' – that are supposed to be available as applications of the Demon hypothesis. Are these thoughts in fact thinkable?

The private language argument and its antecedents in Wittgenstein's thought have always worked against the idea that the surface form of first-person sentences is what it appears to be. Wittgenstein was an early proponent of the view that in first-person sentences like 'I am in pain', 'I' does not refer.[13] Even if this sort of claim captures something important about some first-person sentences, and even if the thinking behind the claim is persuasive, the inclination to say that 'I' sometimes *does* refer is hard to resist. In some exceptional cases, as we shall see, there is even a strong inclination to say that all the 'I' *could* refer to is a Cartesian ego. In short, there appears to be no uniform and satisfactory account of the contribution of the semantic contribution of 'I' to all of the sentences in which it figures. This leaves open the possibility that the Cartesian account captures part of the truth about self-reference even if it does not capture the truth about the central or typical uses of 'I'.

One thing that can be required of any adequate account of first-person sentences about pain is that it state the nature of the asymmetry with third-person sentences. It seems clear that the use of third-person

---

[13] See Hacker, *Insight and Illusion* (Oxford, 1971), ch. 7 for the development of this position in Wittgenstein's writings.

sentences requires an ability to identify and reidentify the referent of 'He' or the relevant proper name; in the first-person case, neither condition holds. One could suffer from amnesia and so not know who one was in the sense required for using one's proper name and yet still use 'I am in pain'; and one does not need to identify a self in order to say that one is in pain. The conditions for using 'I am in pain' might be indistinguishable from those for complying with a doctor's instruction, during an examination, to tell him when it hurts. As soon as the pain starts one can say either 'Now it hurts' or 'I'm in pain', and the truth and assertion conditions might be the same. Considerations like these sometimes underlie so-called "no-ownership" theories of first-person psychological sentences, including the 'I am thinking' of Descartes's *cogito*. According to this sort of theory, 'There is thinking going on' better captures what is assertible in conditions of demonic deception than 'I am thinking', and no Cartesian ego has to exist to make that sentence true. By the same token, no Cartesian ego has to exist to make 'Now it hurts' true either. This sort of approach opens a wide gulf between 'He is in pain' and 'I am in pain', and it must complicate, if not put out of reach, the validation of pieces of reasoning like the following: 'I am in pain and he is in pain; so two people are in pain' and 'I am in pain; so someone is in pain'.

An account which narrows that gulf by allowing that 'I' does refer is Strawson's.[14] Strawson claims that the convention governing the use of the first-person pronoun is the key to understanding the peculiarities of self-reference. This convention is that the pronoun 'I' refers to whoever the user of 'I' is. According to Strawson, first-personal *thoughts* refer to whoever the thinker is by virtue of the same convention: Whoever can have an I-thought has mastered the linguistic practice with the word 'I', and *its* guarantee against reference failure and mistaken reference passes to the 'I' in I-thoughts. No experiences or beliefs or items of knowledge peculiar to the thinker or speaker work to secure reference for 'I' in thought or language, and *what* is referred to standardly is not a Cartesian ego or soul separable from the body and devoid of physical characteristics. The standard referent of 'I' is the *person* one is, in the sense of 'person' made familiar by Strawson's

---

[14] 'The First Person – and Others' in Q. Cassam, ed., *Self-Knowledge* (Oxford: Oxford University Press, 1994), pp. 210–15.

Individuals.[15] A person is an object of reference that is equally open to psychological and physical predicates, and that is not reducible to something that can bear predicates of only one of those types.

So far as standard thought or talk involving the first person is concerned, Strawson is satisfied that the 'I' refers to nothing Cartesian. But he is prepared to consider self-reference in imagined possible situations far removed from the ordinary or even the practically possible. It is in this spirit that he considers who or what is referred to where consciousness seems to be disembodied. This is the sort of case taken up by Anscombe[16] and, following her, Mackie.[17] Strawson does not think that disembodied consciousness is inconceivable, or that 'I' must fail to refer where the thoughts belong to disembodied consciousness. But if the 'I' in an I-thought does refer in this sort of case, it does so by referring to experiences with a source in a Strawsonian person and not a Cartesian ego.[18] One sort of case under discussion comes from Anscombe:

I get into a state of 'sensory deprivation'. Sight is cut off, and I am locally anaesthetised everywhere, perhaps floated in a tank of tepid water. I am unable to speak, or to touch any part of my body with any other. Now I tell myself, 'I won't let this happen again!' If the object meant by 'I' is this body, this human being, then in these circumstances it won't be present to my senses; and how else can it be 'present to' me?

Anscombe asks, 'But have I lost what I mean by "I"'? and expects the answer 'No' – surely correctly. But she thinks it follows from that that 'I' doesn't refer in conditions of sensory deprivation.

Her argument is inconclusive. She runs through the kinds of referring term 'I' could conceivably belong to and gives reasons why it could belong to none. But these reasons are not always compelling.

Why, for example, could 'I' not be a demonstrative pronoun, alongside 'this' or 'that' or phrases like 'this F' or 'that F'? Anscombe's argument is in two parts. First, demonstrative reference by speakers to a thing requires a conception of the thing that answers the question

---

[15] *Individuals – An Essay in Descriptive Metaphysics* (London: Macmillan, 1959), ch. 3.
[16] 'The First Person', reprinted in Cassam, pp. 140–59.
[17] 'The Transcendental "I"' in Z. van Straaten, ed., *Philosophical Subjects* (Oxford, 1980), pp. 48–61.
[18] Strawson in Cassam, op. cit., p. 214.

'This what?'; the conception associated with 'I' is elusive. Second, ordinary demonstratives are liable in unusual cases to reference failure,
while 'I' never is. Neither part of the argument is conclusive. To begin
with reference failure, Anscombe relies on a distinction between what
a demonstrative latches onto and what it refers to. According to her,
a demonstrative must latch on to something, but it can latch onto a
thing other than what it is supposed to refer to, in which case there
are conditions for reference failure. Anscombe explains:

> Someone comes with a box and says, 'This is all that is left of poor Jones'. The
> answer to 'this what?' is 'This parcel of ashes'; but unknown to the speaker
> the box is empty. What 'this' has to have, if used correctly, is something that it
> *latches on to* (as I shall put it): in this example, it is the box. In another example it
> might be an optical presentation. Thus I may ask, 'What's that figure standing
> in front of the rock, a man or a post?' and there may be no such object at all;
> but there is an appearance, a stain perhaps, or other marking on the rock face,
> which my 'that' latches on to. The referent and what 'this' latches onto may
> coincide, as when I say 'This buzzing in my ears is dreadful', or, after listening
> to a speech, 'That was splendid!' But they do not have to coincide, and the
> referent is the object of which the predicate is predicated where 'this' or 'that'
> is the subject.[19]

This is little more than a stipulation that reference failure can only be
the failure of anything present to satisfy the conception that answers
the 'this what?' question. Someone who equated the referent of the
demonstrative with what the demonstrative latched onto would not be
shown to be wrong by anything Anscombe says here, and if 'latching
on' to something and referring might be the same thing, the question
of whether there can be reference failure in cases like those given by
Anscombe remains open.

A corollary is that no distinction between 'I' and 'this' can be erected
in respect to reference failure. On the contrary, cases can easily be
thought up where the conception associated by a suitably deluded
person with 'I' creates conditions for an exact counterpart of 'reference failure'. Suppose I suffer from a mental illness that makes me
think I am Napoleon, and I say, as if to a subordinate at the Battle of
Austerlitz, 'I order you to attack at daybreak'. The counterpart of the
'this what?' question is the 'I what or who?'. And the answer to it is 'I,

[19] Anscombe in Cassam, pp. 148–9.

Napoleon' or 'I, the commander'. That conception is not satisfied by anyone at the time or place I say, 'I order you to attack at daybreak'; so there appears to be reference failure in something like Anscombe's sense; but the 'I' *does* latch on to something, namely me. So far, 'I' and 'this' are on a par.

Anscombe has a second line of thought intended as a reductio of the interpretation of 'I' as a demonstrative; this comments on the source of the guarantee against reference failure with 'I':

> We saw that there may be reference failure for 'this', in that one may mean 'this parcel of ashes' when there are no ashes. But 'I' – if it makes a reference, if, that is, its mode of meaning is that it is supposed to make a reference – is secure against reference-failure. Just thinking 'I . . .' guarantees not only the exist-ence but the presence of its referent. It guarantees the existence *because* it guarantees the presence, which is presence to consciousness. But NB, here 'presence to consciousness' means physical or real presence, not just that one is thinking of the thing. For, if the thinking did not guarantee the presence, the existence of the referent could be doubted. . . . Whether 'I' is a name or a demonstrative, there is the same need of a 'conception' through which it attaches to its object. Now what conception can be suggested, other than that of thinking, the thinking of the I-thought, which secures this guarantee against reference-failure.[20]

Anscombe looks for a conception to associate with 'I' that is guaran-teed to be satisfied when 'I' is used, a conception that determines the reference. But awareness or consciousness, as in episodes of pain, does not depend on reference-determining conceptions, and why can't that awareness or consciousness, which is always awareness to a self, guaran-tee presence, and suffice for a latching on of the 'I'? Why can't latching on, rather than reference-via-conception, be all that is guaranteed? It is true that not all awareness is sensory awareness, as it is in episodes of pain. When I reflect that I am thinking of the Eiffel Tower, I do not feel anything, but the Eiffel Tower is still something I'm aware of, and it is not only pictured by me; it is presented to me. Because the awareness is awareness for or to a subject, there is conscious presence. Presence to a subject is quite different from a subject's arriving in the Cartesian way at the *conclusion* that an image of the Eiffel Tower is someone's im-age, and in particular his image, based on the premisses that here is an

---

[20] Ibid., p. 149.

image of the Eiffel Tower, images must be had by someone, and there *is* no one else. No *reflection* or reasoning gets the image of the Eiffel Tower to function as my image of the Eiffel Tower. At the same time, no conception of myself seems to come into it either. So we have latching on rather than a case of the sense of 'I' guiding the term to its referent.

Now in the sensory deprivation case the conditions for a latching on still exist, because the subject is presumably still able to think of the Eiffel Tower. What is missing is a whole range of experience and awareness, namely of bodily movement, bodily shape, bodily position, pain, and so on. This range of experience may be very important for getting both self-reference and psychological predicates into a given speaker's vocabulary, for this experience has connections with a wide range of behaviours that are cues for the application of the predicates by observers, and so cues for observers-cum-teachers of the language to introduce the predicates into the subject's vocabulary. In Anscombe's sensory deprivation case, the sources of both bodily sensation and the corresponding behaviour are blocked off in a single subject who is linguistically competent. The fact that self-reference is still possible for a speaker in conditions of sensory deprivation does not show that bodily sensations and behaviour aren't essential for learning to use 'I' and psychological predicates in the first place. On the contrary, it is perfectly plausible to say that self-ascriptions of pain have to be a possibility for a speaker before self-ascriptions of thoughts or images of the Eiffel Tower are. By the same token, the fact that self-reference and self-awareness are still possible after sensory deprivation does not show that self-reference is possible independent of the existence of bodily sensations or their connection with behaviour. The use of 'I' might be compared in this respect with the use of some numeral words. The numeral '10' does not mean the number of fingers that a single human being normally has, but the fact that people normally have ten fingers each may be important to the human ability to refer to and calculate with the number 10. Similarly, 'I' does not mean 'this body' or 'this human being' and self-reference is possible for a human being cut off from experience of her body, but experience of one's body and its normal effects in behaviour are surely conditions of the human capacity for self-reference.

Descartes, of course, did not deny that embodiment was important to learning how to use 'I'. He did not even deny that 'I' is sometimes,

emotion or episodes of locomotion as by awareness of doubt. It is a Cartesian ego in the minimal sense of something that has states of awareness, states that secure a latching on for the 'I' in first-person sentences expressing those awarenesses. Not every state of the subject secures this latching on. The activity of my digestive system or cell activity within my brain are activities in me, but they don't register with me. And it is being a state that occurs within me *and* registers with me that secures the latching on of the 'I'.

On my minimally Cartesian view of first-person sentences about sensation and thought, the first-person pronoun refers, in the sense of latching on to, a necessarily present self. Reference does not take place by an object's fitting a conception associated with or synonymous with 'I'. An associated conception or sense is not what guarantees presence. But presence *is* important. The self-implicatingness of some sensations and emotions and some thoughts does play a role in the account. In Strawson, there is apparently no role for presence. The linguistic convention for pronominal self-reference is all the explanation one needs or gets of why 'I' refers to me. According to me, the operation of the convention takes place against the background of the self-implicatingness of certain states. But I do not take self-implicatingness to be involved in all thought, still less all mental states, and I do not suppose it contributes *directly* to all self-reference. If I come across an entry in my diary that records an incident I can't remember, and I infer from the language that I must have been very upset, I am going by the expression of the upset rather than the experience or memory of the experience. But self-implicatingness probably did contribute to the self-reference as the lines in the diary were being written. So perhaps self-intimatingness contributes to, or is a condition even of, my reconstruction of what I once felt through its expression.

SELF-IMPLICATINGNESS AND FIRST-PERSON AUTHORITY

The minimally Cartesian view that I am attracted to may coincide with Shoemaker's view,[22] according to which self-reference depends on

---

[22] 'Self-Reference and Self-Awareness' in Shoemaker's collection, *Identity, Cause and Mind: Philosophical Essays* (Cambridge: Cambridge University Press, 1984), pp. 6–18.

the existence of psychological predicates with the following defining characteristic: They can apply in a special way to subjects, such that, when they apply that way, the subjects cannot fail to know they do. 'Is in pain' is such a predicate. Shoemaker calls these P* predicates, and he thinks that these predicates are the sort that are self-ascribed in cases Wittgenstein calls uses of 'I' as subject: 'I see so-and so'; 'I am trying to lift my arm'; and so on. Wittgenstein contrasts uses of 'I' as subject with uses of 'I' as object, where a reference to one's body can take the place of 'I', as in 'I have grown six inches' or 'I can't get into these trousers'. Shoemaker argues persuasively that uses of 'I' as object depend on uses of 'I' as subject, for many of those uses will be references by the use of 'I' to a certain body, which has to be known to be *mine* for me to assert that it has grown six inches or that it is too big for these trousers, and this will be a matter of knowing predicates like 'can see over X's head' and 'can feel legs being squeezed', which, have to be self-ascribed to apply to one's body.

It was the example of pain that led us to questions of self-reference and P* predicates. Descartes says that the perception of pain is clear in the sense that the pain is unmistakeable and inescapable to the mind's eye. It is natural to take this for an explanation of why for him one can't be mistaken that one is in pain. In fact, Descartes doesn't take the clarity of pain to explain the impossibility of mistake in the first-person case. The clarity perhaps explains the spontaneity and irresistibility of assent to 'I am in pain'. But he thinks that we need to have some extra reason for thinking that what a mind assents to in that way couldn't be false. He assumes that if a mind *were* deceived in this state, it would be deceived despite its best efforts to avoid the main sources of human error: the habit of jumping to conclusions and the indistinctness of perception arising from embodiment. Falling into error despite doing everything humanly possible to avoid it would be nothing less than extreme cognitive unfairness, which is excluded if the creator of the mind is no deceiver and would not have given us a faculty of perception that inclines us to falsehood (*Principles* I, 43: AT IXB 21; CSM I 207). Descartes does purport to prove that the creator of the mind is no deceiver. The conclusion of this proof, rather than the associations of the metaphor of the all-seeing inner eye, is the basis of Descartes's explanation of the impossibility of error in many first-person cases. And it is this conclusion that ties together the certainty of entertaining a certain thought to the compellingness of '2 + 2 = 4' or 'God exists'. Or 'material bodies exist'.

The Cartesian approach, then, does not depend on investing the first-person perspective, or truths expressed in the first person, with a special *intrinsic* authority. The compellingness of certain truths to the attentive mind, though it is necessarily a compellingness *for* a self, could be the sign of demonic manipulation unless we can be sure that something about the constitution of the mind rules out basic error. This impersonally true consideration is that God makes the mind and constitutes it to know the general attributes – thought and extension – of things and the modes of these attributes. The ideas of mental and physical substance, attribute and mode are all part of its innate endowment. It is true that for Descartes knowledge of the attribute of thought, with its connection to the first person, has a certain preeminence. Unlike knowledge of extension, knowledge of thought is inalienable in the face of extreme doubt; but knowledge does not have to be inalienable to be knowledge, and what knowledge of the modes of extension and the modes of thought have in common, namely knowledge of how they depend on extension and thought and, beyond those things, God's nature, may be more important than what divides them. (This may be the message of Spinoza's departure from Descartes, if it *is* a departure.) Under the conjecture of the demonic doubt, the dependences on the mental side stand out and are registered first-personally, but in general they do not need to be, and 'It has parts; so it is extended' is as clear and distinct, other things being equal, as 'I doubt; so I think'.

The inner arena explanation of immunity from error, then, actually depends on the benign creator explanation of immunity from error, and it is the benign creator explanation that allows for certainty *wherever* assent is spontaneous in an attentive mind – that is, in regard to truths about matter and mathematics as opposed to current psychological states.

2

Knowledge, the Self, and Internalism

There is a difference between a theory of knowledge that starts from a sceptically impregnable inner space and a theory of knowledge which insists that a first-person perspective is ineliminable and important to the theory of knowledge. Both sorts of approaches probably qualify as 'Cartesian' in some sense, but the second has no particular associations with solipsism or privacy. It works with a category of things directly evident to the self, but it does not have to define the directly evident as the residue of applying the method of doubt, and it can count some things as directly evident that would not survive the uncertainty of Meditation One. It implies that consciousness matters to epistemology, but it does not make consciousness disembodied or require that any one consciousness be cut off from other minds. Versions of this sort of approach are adopted by 'internalists' in the debate in analytic epistemology between internalism and externalism. Internalists hold, roughly, that the difference between true belief and knowledge depends on something accessible to consciousness of the knower – the reasons he accepts, say, rather than the kind of causal origins the true belief had outside the believer. The argument of this chapter is that there is something right in internalism and that no purely externalist approach to the theory of knowledge can be entirely satisfactory. This is the innocent Cartesianism in analytic epistemology.

THE AUTONOMY OF KNOWING AND THE
'PREJUDICES OF CHILDHOOD'

To motivate innocent Cartesianism, it helps to start with Descartes himself. A good source for his general views about the way knowledge involves the self is a letter he wrote in October 1630 to Isaac Beeckman, the mentor of his earliest years as an intellectual. In the letter, Descartes responds sharply to Beeckman's suggestion that Beeckman had taught Descartes a great deal:

> [I]f someone merely comes to believe something, without being swayed by any authority or argument, which he has learnt from others, this does not mean that he has been taught it by anyone, even though he may have heard many people say it. It may even happen that he really knows it, being impelled to believe it by true reasons, and that no one before him has ever known it, although they may have been of the same opinion, because they deduced it from false principles. . . . Have I ever been moved by your authority? Have I ever been convinced by your arguments? Well, you said, I believed and accepted some of your views as soon as I understood them. But, mark you, the fact that I believed them at once does not show that I learnt them from you; I accepted them, rather, because I had already arrived at the same views myself. . . . Many people can know the same thing without any of them having learnt it from the others. It is ridiculous to take the trouble as you do to distinguish, in the possession of knowledge, what is your own from what is not, as if it was the possession of a piece of land or sum of money. If you know something, it is completely yours, even if you learnt it from someone else. (AT I 158; CSM III 27)

The deeply characteristic view that Descartes is expressing here is to the effect that to know is never vicarious or passive: Knowledge is not something that befalls one but results from the acceptance of things after having weighed reasons for them. Things one is 'taught', on the other hand, especially when the teaching is taken in uncritically and turns one into the mouthpiece for the sayings of some sage or academic celebrity, need not be known even when they are true: They need to be *made* one's own by being understood and accepted for reasons one has thought through oneself.

Elsewhere, as in the *Discourse* or the *Meditations*, the message is similar. Really to know something is not only to be 'involved', but to be personally *active*, in acquiring true beliefs or, short of this, in deciding to retain them. We might call what Descartes is insisting upon 'the autonomy of knowing'. Although many beliefs are in fact acquired unthinkingly in perception and through testimony or from a cultural tradition, the fact that they are unthinkingly acquired is, according to Descartes, a sort of defect even if the beliefs are true. What would happen if they were to be challenged, or if someone made a persuasive case for contrary and false beliefs? In such a case we might not, probably *would* not, know what to think. And this is probably true for all of the time our beliefs happen to escape challenge or persuasive competition: At the same time as we believe, we are in danger of being reduced to not knowing what to think. What is more, we can be conscious of this. In a sense, we believe gratuitously. The remedy for this is to reconsider as many beliefs as possible, or to adopt good criteria for acceptance of things to believe, criteria that will pick out the true, or at least pick out the true more often than the false. Both of these things – critical reconsideration and the suggestion of new criteria for acceptance – are attempted on a grand scale in the *Meditations*. Nothing less than the whole edifice of preexisting belief is supposed to be reconsidered critically and selectively retained.

This makes the requirements of knowledge very exacting, implausibly exacting, according to externalists. Surely some knowledge *is* a sort of unthinking by-product of the ordinary operation of sensory and memory mechanisms. It is not all autonomously arrived at. Descartes may be right to insist that some knowledge is autonomous; he may be right in thinking that a lot of knowledge can and should be more autonomous, but he seems wrong to hold that all knowledge is autonomous. There is also Descartes's psychologistic understanding of the sort of certainty that marks autonomous knowledge: the power of making a particular psychological impact on a mind trained to be attentive. It may not be the clarity and distinctness of the thought 'bodies exist' in the light of the proof of Meditation Six that makes it certain, as Descartes claims, but perhaps something else.

In this connection it pays to take account of Descartes's general theory of *Meditations* and elsewhere, that many of the beliefs we unthinkingly hold are mere preconceptions of our childhood. For example, when he says at the beginning of Part Two of the *Principles* that everyone's belief in the existence of an external world is a preconceived belief of childhood (AT VIIIA 40; CSM I 223), this refers to a theory of preconceptions that he developed earlier. In sections at the end of Part One of the *Principles* (§§ 71ff) that are rarely quoted, Descartes speculatively reconstructs the natural origin of the misuse of sensory information to tell us about the natures of external things. In early childhood the 'mind was so closely tied to the body that it had no leisure for any thoughts except those by means of which it had sensory awareness of what was happening to the body. What was beneficial or harmful was felt only as pleasure or pain in the body' (AT VIIIA 35; CSM I 218). It is only when the child moves its body and learns to pursue the beneficial and avoid the harmful that it starts to attribute an independent existence to the things outside its body, and to refer the colours, smells, and tastes it experiences, as well as shapes and sizes, to those external things. 'Moreover, since the mind judged everything in terms of its utility to the body in which it was immersed, it assessed the amount of reality in each object by the extent to which it was affected by it.' It is in this way, Descartes says, that we come to think that rocks and metals are more substantial or real or material than water or air. The key to seeing the natures of things aright is withdrawal from the body – acquiring a capacity for judgement that does not assign natures to external objects in relation to how they can harm or benefit us. Detaching ourselves from the body is partly a matter of seeing that judgements inspired mainly by our involvement with our bodies are uncertain or erroneous. The most extreme and radical form of this detachment is achieved by the radical doubt practised by Descartes in Meditation One.

Not only the natures of things but also their existence look different after detachment. The proof of the existence of material things in Meditation Six is a world away from the childhood phenomenon of first moving one's body around, but both are supposed to produce a belief in an external world. The proof produces the belief in such a way as to assure that it is *scientia*; moving about as a child produces something far inferior – not real knowledge at all but maybe something like animal belief in the existence of external things. It is here, in connection with Descartes's depiction of the process by which the animal belief is produced, and in connection with the belief that there can be, and ought to be, personal, reason-based knowledge that external bodies exist – it is here that some of Wittgenstein's insights in *On Certainty* seem apposite and illuminating. It may be, as Wittgenstein says, and Descartes would deny, that there is *no* better grasp of the truth that bodies exist than an animal belief in it (cf. *OC§§* 475ff); and the conditions for proving *anything* and knowing *anything* may depend on the fact that 'bodies exist' and other truths like it are beyond proof and beyond knowledge in some sense.

Certainly 'bodies exist' and some other truths can be supposed to be beyond *personal* knowledge (*OC§§* 252; 440). To the extent anyone can be certain of them, everyone has to be certain of them. The idea that there is one kind of acceptance of them that consists of simple unthinking absorption, and another, better sort of acceptance that depends on consciousness of reasons for them, and that counts as scientia, is simply a misconception, according to Wittgenstein, traceable to a misunderstanding of the different roles that certain quasi-propositions play in life and schemes of belief. Rather than being learnt by each person as he makes his way in pursuit of the beneficial and away from the harmful, these propositions may never be learnt at all. Instead, according to Wittgenstein, they are attempts to articulate the things that have to be taken for granted if much that we do with and say about material objects is to make sense. For example, when Descartes allows himself out of the confines of the doubt in Meditation Two and forms the sense-based conception of the piece of wax, attributing properties to it on the basis of handling and knocking the wax, these ways of acting on the wax take for granted that bodies exist (cf. *OC§* 285) – even if the thought of their existence is never formulated. Suspending the presupposition that bodies exist, accordingly, is more than a matter of trying to take seriously the dream and Demon hypotheses: It means opting out of a large-scale way of acting – a form of life – that, if Wittgenstein is right, cannot be opted out of while leaving everything else – for example, the meanings of 'wax', 'soft', 'melts' – undisturbed.

These points of Wittgenstein's are well taken, and though I doubt that they were arrived at with Descartes in mind,[1] they do count against Descartes's classification of our pre-rational belief that bodies exist as a sort of prejudice that needs to purged along with other badly supported or unreasonable beliefs. In a way Descartes agrees about the special status of 'bodies exist'. He never claims that it is comparable

---

[1] They are directed, instead, or at least in part, at the theory of tautological certainty in Wittgenstein's *Tractatus Logico-Philosophicus*. I have substantiated this view in an unpublished Oxford B.Phil. thesis, 'Knowledge and Meaning (with special reference to Wittgenstein)' (1975).

to 'heavenly bodies are unchanging', which *is* a prejudiced assertion arising from taking Aristotelian cosmology as gospel. Again, he acknowledges a distinction between hypotheses that can be contested in ordinary life and ordinary science, and propositions that one needs to reconsider only once in a lifetime. He distinguishes between propositions that are called into question by a merely temporary metaphysical doubt, and much more dubitable propositions about the causes of storms or the basis of the transmission of light. He acknowledges, too, that the acceptance of 'bodies exist' is more fundamental to our life – bound up as it is with the most primitive kinds of human locomotion – than propositions about, for example, the makeup of coal. What he denies – probably mistakenly – is that any propositions lie out of the reach of reasons of some kind or other. And he insists, probably mistakenly again, that when propositions do lie outside the reach of reasons, they need to be dropped or rejected or replaced, when believers are old enough, with something better.

Another way of putting the lesson of On *Certainty* for Descartes is by saying that the method of doubt misclassifies many things that we think without reason as things we think gratuitously, or things we think heteronomously, suspending our powers of judgement in the face of intellectual authority or not exercising our powers of detachment from the beliefs that are induced with the use of our senses. 'Bodies exist' does not fit in this way of thinking. It is not a truth we *can* hit upon on our own. Taking its truth for granted is not, then, a case of heteronomy.

EXTERNALISM AND REFLECTIVENESS

Even if not all of the beliefs that we acquire or retain unthinkingly *could* have been acquired thinkingly, many are in principle open to critical examination followed by acceptance or rejection. If a belief *can* be accepted or rejected on the basis of critical reflection, then *shouldn't* it be? Isn't it better that it be accepted or rejected reflectively than that it be accepted or rejected for no reason that the believer can think of? Descartes's answer to this question in the case of the data and explanations of natural science is a resounding 'Yes', and the second-nature rationalism that I referred to in the Introduction may seem to generalise this answer to all the beliefs we can think twice about, including ones far outside natural science, like the belief that a certain film or restaurant is particularly good. Externalism in analytic epistemology implies, to the contrary, that critical reflection is not always necessary. It is not necessary for a belief to amount to *knowledge*, and if knowledge is the highest status a belief can achieve, externalism implies that critical reflection does not always matter to belief in its best form.

In one prominent form, externalism holds that the difference between true belief and knowledge is to do with the mechanisms and causes of belief outside the head, and their tendency to produce true rather than false belief. Externalism recognises for example sense perception and testimony as typical sources of true belief and lays down conditions that the uses of the senses and reliance on informants must satisfy to produce true belief reliably. It is distinctive of an externalist analysis that the conditions it lays down can be satisfied without the subject's being aware that they are. Not only do externalist analyses deny that when one knows, one knows that one knows, but they also imply that mechanisms for belief production do not have to involve the consciousness of the subject, still less a conscious process of weighing reasons, in order that the beliefs produced be true or amount to knowledge. For example, identificatory knowledge – knowing who or which a given person or thing is – can involve discriminatory capacities in perceivers that they are not aware are being exercised. Knowledge based on testimony can be a matter of hearing something true from an authoritative source, without the subject's being aware that or why the source is authoritative.

I think externalism must capture part of the truth about the concept of knowledge. This concept can apply even when critical reflection is quite out of its element: Babies and dogs can know things because their states of belief can be produced, unbeknownst to them, in ways that make it no accident that what is believed is true. Even unconscious beliefs can be knowledge-ranking, as in the case of true arithmetical beliefs that would not be held in the absence of the believer's mastery of the times tables. But the fact that it makes sense to attribute knowledge or true belief to subjects who are unreflective or incapable of reflection does not mean that critical reflectiveness is not a desideratum in those who *can* reflect. One reason is that the capacity for reflection is itself a source of instability of belief. As soon as one can appreciate a conflict between one's beliefs, as one does when evidence one believes is discovered to go against other things one believes, one stands under a rational requirement to abandon beliefs and restore consistency. Knowing that one must abandon some beliefs, but not knowing which, one can even give up those that were produced in ways appropriate for believing truths. This is why being able to adjudicate conflicts through critical reflection can be epistemically desirable: because the alternative seems to be irrational wilful blindness to counter-evidence or widespread suspension of belief, sometimes amounting to loss of knowledge. One can of course be spared particular challenges to one's beliefs, so that the need for critical reflection does not present itself in practice. But the sceptical hypotheses of traditional epistemology show that in theory the need for being able to come up with reasons for what one believes is inescapable. Epistemology itself provides very general reasons for thinking twice about nearly all one's beliefs, and there is no incompatibility between acknowledging this and acknowledging the truth in externalism. The fact that the concept of knowledge does not require reflectiveness or a capacity for critical reflection in every knowing subject with respect to every thing believed does not mean that there is no problem of the form 'Should I hold the beliefs I hold?'

Sometimes this last point is missed, because of a clash of two research programmes in analytic epistemology. One is the age-old programme of finding a criterion of truth and an answer to epistemological scepticism. The other is the programme of finding a solution to the Gettier puzzle – that is, of stating conditions necessary and sufficient for factual knowledge that are proof against counter-examples that discredit knowledge as justified true belief. Especially in externalist hands, there is a tension between these two programmes. There is a tension even if one thinks that epistemological scepticism is to the effect that we do not know anything. For it does not answer the conjecture that perhaps we do not know anything to be told what it is to know something. Even if satisfactory necessary and sufficient conditions for knowledge could be stated, the statement would hardly establish that they were ever satisfied. And conditions for *knowledge* may be beside the point. Scepticism is just as reasonably expressed by asking whether there is any reason for anyone to *believe* anything or make any judgement. Externalist analyses of knowledge leave *this* sort of question entirely untouched. A subject who has no idea how or why he believes what he does, but who nevertheless, unbeknownst to him, has a true belief and one produced in a way that is reliable for arriving at truths, has nothing to counterbalance the hypothesis that perhaps he is dreaming or being deceived by a demon. So even if he knows, it is not a knowledge that rules out the rational unsettlement of belief.

It would be open to the externalist to agree that the analysis of knowledge or the solution of the Gettier puzzle is not all there is to epistemology, but that it is the analysis of knowledge and the solution of the Gettier puzzle that concerns him. Success with this does not refute scepticism; on the contrary, it may help to reveal why scepticism arises. If on the basis of our grasp of the concept of knowledge we can make sense of the possibility that we know nothing, then there is nothing wrong with an externalist analysis of knowledge following suit and laying down conditions of knowledge that permit or even invite scepticism as to whether they are satisfied. Thus, it is open to the externalist to say that just because so much that goes into the formation of belief eludes us by depending on things outside consciousness or even outside the head altogether, we can never be sure that, unbeknownst to us, undermining conditions are not being satisfied – like the production of belief by a deceiving demon. But externalists do not often say this. Typically, they are anti-sceptical, and they seem to take any scepticism-inviting consequences of proposed analyses of knowledge to be reductios of those proposals. Sometimes they endorse the Quinean programme of naturalising epistemology, which unapologetically substitutes live empirical questions about the processes of belief formation for (as they think) stale armchair questions about the justification of belief.

A representative of the anti-sceptical and naturalising tendency in externalism is Alvin Goldman. In a series of writings dating back to the 1960s that started with the proposal of a causal theory of knowledge, Goldman has been one of the most consistent advocates of empirically informed accounts of belief-forming mechanisms, and one of the harshest critics of theories of justification that are both aprioristic and tied to a strong thesis of the conscious accessibility of reasons for belief necessary for knowledge. In a relatively recent paper criticising internalist theories of knowledge,[2] Goldman argues as if the scepticism-inviting character of internalist commitments were virtually a refutation of those commitments. He writes,

Strong internalism threatens a drastic diminution in the stock of beliefs ordinarily deemed justified, and hence in the stock of knowledge, assuming that justification is necessary for knowledge. This is a major count against this type of theory.[3]

And a little later:

A crippling problem emerges for internalism. If epistemic principles are not knowable by naïve agents, no such principles can qualify as justifiers.... If no epistemic principles so qualify, any agent can justifiably believe no propositions. Wholescale skepticism follows.[4]

Goldman is not claiming, I think, that 'wholescale scepticism' is actually entailed by internalism, only that, on some natural assumptions, our commonsense conviction that we have many reasonable beliefs and quite a lot of knowledge will be challenged or denied. But why should this commonsense conviction have any authority within epistemology? Isn't it precisely one of the beliefs contested within the subject? It is true that some intuitions ought to be preserved by the analysis of knowledge, namely intuitions about when it is appropriate to credit subjects with knowledge as opposed to mere true belief: The analysis of knowledge is after all answerable to our use of 'knowledge-that'. But like other pieces of linguistic analysis, it should state what conditions are fulfilled if and only if someone knows that *p*. It need not and should not decide whether any of these conditions are actually fulfilled, or work on the assumption that they usually are. On the contrary, fitting as it does into the branch of philosophy traditionally defined by the problem of scepticism, an analysis of knowledge should not be guided by the assumption that the problem is bogus because it disturbs common sense. It should permit scepticism to be coherently statable, if only because the concept of knowledge

---

[2] 'Internalism Exposed', *Journal of Philosophy* 96 (1999), pp. 271–93.
[3] Ibid., p. 278.
[4] Ibid., p. 288.

may itself have sceptically questionable presuppositions,[5] and it should leave it to further argument to decide whether scepticism is ill founded or not.[6]

Barry Stroud has suggested that anti-sceptical externalism might be a certain sort of explanatory enterprise, one that sets out to vindicate, without taking for granted, our commonsense belief that we know things. With the version of externalism proposed by Ernest Sosa in mind,[7] he writes,

We aspire in philosophy to see ourselves as knowing all or most of the things we think we know and to understand how all that knowledge is possible. We want an explanation, not just of this or that item or piece of knowledge, but of knowledge, or knowledge of a certain kind, *in general*. Take all our knowledge of the world of physical objects around us, for example. A satisfactory "theory" or explanation of that knowledge must have several features. To be satisfyingly positive, it must depict us as knowing all or most of the things of the sort that we think we know. It must explain, given what it takes to be the facts of human perception, how we nonetheless know the sorts of things we think we know about the world. To say simply that we see, hear, and touch the things around us and in that way know what they are like would leave nothing even initially problematic about that knowledge. Rather than explaining how, it would simply state that we know. There is nothing wrong with that; it is true, but it does not explain how we know even in those cases in which (as we would say) we are in fact seeing or hearing or touching an object. That is what we want in a philosophical explanation of our knowledge. . . . What needs explanation is the connection between perceiving what we do and our knowing things we

---

[5] In *Descartes: The Project of Pure Enquiry* (Harmondsworth: Penguin, 1978), pp. 64–5, Williams suggests that the concept of knowledge may carry commitment to the problematic idea of the absolute conception.

[6] In Chapter 1 of *Epistemology and Cognition* (Cambridge, Mass.: Harvard University Press, 1986), Goldman is officially more tolerant of scepticism. He is sympathetic to the realism that gives rise to scepticism and is critical of lines of thought to the effect that sceptical theses cannot coherently be stated, or that they can be answered by reductionist theses (p. 34) or transcendental arguments (p. 36). He also claims that analyses of epistemic concepts can be relevant to answering scepticism. But he insists that scepticism is only one problem in epistemology among others (p. 39), and that even if it cannot be refuted, there is still a point to a theory of or analysis of reliability in belief-producing processes. Because this is consistent with leaving open the question of whether scepticism is tenable philosophically, I have less of an objection to it than to the scepticism-dismissing tendency of 'Internalism Exposed'. Less of an objection rather than no objection. Scepticism is not one concern among others in epistemology, but the central concern.

[7] 'Philosophical Scepticism and Epistemic Circularity', *Proceedings of the Aristotelian Society(s.v)*, 1994. Sosa thinks that at best a theory can make us confident that the processes by which we arrive at our beliefs are reliable.

do about the physical objects around us. How does the one lead to, or amount to, the other?[8]

Stroud goes on to suggest that no externalist theory will provide anyone with a satisfactory understanding of his own knowledge, because, in order for the theory to seem satisfactory, the subject has to be sure that his *own* knowledge is acquired in the way externalism requires, and (if I understand Stroud) there is nothing self-intimating about that way of acquiring knowledge. The subject may have knowledge, and have knowledge in virtue of his beliefs being true and being underpinned by reliable cognitive mechanisms, and yet those facts about belief-formation not register with him, so that is still an open question for him whether he does understand his knowledge.[9]

It looks as if what creates the problem is the tension between externalism, with its distinctive disregard for the first-person perspective, and the need for a first-person registration of the fact that one's beliefs are underpinned by reliable mechanisms if one is to understand one's own knowledge. For his part, Stroud says that the real problem is that of wishing to have any theory of knowledge in general, in the sense of 'theory' explained in the passage just quoted. Such a theory requires, in the case of physical objects, that things we know about physical objects be derivable from a theory telling us about human perception. But, Stroud says, there is no separating off the things we know about physical objects and the way perception works, as if the latter could be understood independently of, and in that sense explain in a strong sense, what we know about physical objects.[10]

I think the source of the problem is rather different. Externalism uses the resources of cognitive and social psychology to give a general picture of reliable mechanisms for forming true beliefs, but, *pace* Sosa, this does not increase our confidence in the truth of most of our beliefs in the face of philosophical scepticism, because philosophical

---

[8] 'Scepticism, "Externalism", and Epistemology', in Stroud's collection of essays, *Understanding Human Knowledge* (Oxford: Oxford University Press, 2000), p. 145.

[9] Ibid., p. 150.

[10] 'I think the source [of the not-fully-satisfiable demand embodied in the epistemological question of how knowledge is possible] lies somewhere within the familiar and powerful line of thinking by which all our alleged knowledge of the world gets even temporarily split off all at once from what we get I perception, so that we are presented with a completely general question about our knowledge of the world to answer' (p. 153).

scepticism calls into question the methods and results of cognitive psychology just as much as the ordinary beliefs that are supposed to result from the mechanisms that cognitive psychology postulates or uncovers. Cognitive psychology contributes not to the answer to scepticism, but to the elaboration of the 'non-accidentally' or 'reliable mechanism' in the formula 'knowledge is non-accidentally true belief' or 'knowledge is true belief produced by a reliable mechanism'. Some of the perplexity felt and diagnosed by Stroud and Sosa arises directly from the conflation of the two distinct projects of answering the sceptic and analysing knowledge-that.

'META-EPISTEMOLOGY' VERSUS 'NORMATIVE EPISTEMOLOGY'

It is sometimes thought that that, while distinct, the projects of analysing knowledge and answering scepticism are related systematically, indeed related as meta-ethics is related to normative ethics. Normative ethics is the theory that tries to justify systematically a range of judgements concerning what we ought and ought not to do, and meta-ethics provides the analysis of concepts, for example the concepts of right, wrong, duty, welfare, practical reason, respect, person – called upon in normative ethics in the process of justification. In the same way, there is supposed to be a theory that justifies a range of judgements about when things are known or justifiably believed, a theory that corresponds to normative ethics, and another theory – meta-epistemology – that analyses the relevant concepts. In ethics, the questions and answers of normative ethics are the raw material of meta-ethics. For the most part meta-ethics assumes that the questions and answers make sense. A meta-ethical position which implied that the whole normative ethical enterprise was misguided or incoherent – arguably the upshot of nihilism – might be criticisable as an anti–meta-ethics, rather than as a contribution to meta-ethics.

Richard Fumerton has claimed that externalism is a meta-epistemological position that compromises normative epistemology in its justificatory work in the face of scepticism, and that therefore a version of internalism is to be preferred to externalism.[11] Although

---

[11] *Metaepistemology and Skepticism* (Lanham, Md.: Rowman and Littlefield, 1995).

Fumerton does not claim that externalism compromises normative epistemology in the way nihilism compromises normative ethics, he does think that externalism begs the question at issue between sceptics and anti-sceptics, and, according to Fumerton, it is undesirable for meta-epistemology to prejudice questions in normative epistemology. As should already be clear, I agree that externalists often take the short way with scepticism, but I reject the analogy between meta-ethics and meta-epistemology. I regard the project of analysing knowledge-that as a relic of a time when the medium of philosophy was philosophical analysis, understood as statements of necessary and sufficient conditions in answer to 'What-is-it?' questions.[12] Although no one any longer practices philosophical analysis, understood that way, on philosophically important concepts like truth or causation or free agency, necessary and sufficient conditions for knowledge-that have continued to be proposed under the stimulus of a recalcitrant Gettier paradox. The traditional epistemological question that came closest to fitting this sort of analysis was the question of the difference between true belief and knowledge, not that of scepticism. But the question of true belief *versus* knowledge is not nearly as central to epistemology as the sceptical question of whether we have reason to believe anything or make judgements or assertions about anything; still less is it a *version* of the sceptical question. So if scepticism defines the preoccupations of a normative epistemology, and if the task of a would-be meta-epistemology is to analyse the concepts required to answer scepticism as a whole or scepticisms with respect to particular subject matters – the external world, other minds, the past, and so on – the analysis of knowledge does not seem to me to contribute to meta-epistemology. Or at least, it fails to contribute to a meta-epistemology that is credibly comparable to meta-ethics.

Fumerton is nevertheless right to suggest that externalism does not do justice, and perhaps *cannot* do justice, to epistemological scepticism. He is right to suggest this, though his argument leaves a lot to be desired. The argument runs as follows: Externalism may be right to claim against the sceptic that a lot of non-inferential true belief is due to reliable mechanisms and is therefore, contrary to scepticism, well-justified belief or knowledge. But to the extent that this claim can

---

[12] See my article on the analysis of knowledge in G. H. R. Parkinson, ed., *The Encyclopaedia of Philosophy* (London: Routledge, 1988), pp. 127–39.

be borne out against the sceptic, it cannot be borne out *philosophically*, because the questions of which mechanisms are reliable and which mechanism underpins non-inferential beliefs are empirical or scientific questions. So if externalism is true, the answer to scepticism is largely extra-philosophical or scientific, contrary to the tradition.[13] As Fumerton puts it,

Philosophers as they are presently trained have no *philosophical* expertise enabling them to reach conclusions about which beliefs are or are not justified. Since the classic issues of scepticism fall under normative epistemology, it follows that if externalism were correct, philosophers should simply stop addressing the questions raised by the sceptic. The complex causal conditions that determine the presence or absence of justification for a belief are the subject matter of empirical investigations that would take the philosopher out of the easy chair and into the laboratory.[14]

The laboratory enterprise would consist of identifying the mechanisms involved in memory and perception when they produce true beliefs. But, Fumerton, asks, wouldn't these investigations invite sceptical questions in turn? Wouldn't it be open to the sceptic to ask, about any mechanism proposed as conferring reliability on perception or memory, how it is *known* or reasonably believed to be such a mechanism? Fumerton says that externalism would still apply. It would say that

If reliablism is true, and if perception happens to be a reliable process, we could perceive various facts about our sense organs and the way they respond to the external world. Again, *if* reliabilism is true, and *if* memory is reliable, we could use memory to justify our belief that memory is reliable.[15]

Fumerton goes on to suggest that this would involve reliabilism in particular and externalism in general in a 'blatant, indeed pathetic, circularity'. In general,

[t]he very ease with which externalists can deal with the sceptical challenge [at the level of justifying their belief in the reliability of proposed reliable mechanisms] betrays the ultimate implausibility of externalism as an attempt to explicate concepts that are of *philosophical* interest. If a philosopher starts

---

[13] For more on the way in which externalism departs from or disrupts traditional epistemology, see L. Bonjour, 'Externalist Theories of Empirical Knowledge', *Midwest Studies in Philosophy* 5 (1980), p. 56.

[14] *Metaepistemology and Skepticism*, op. cit., p. 171.

[15] Ibid., p. 173.

wondering about the reliability of astrological inference, the philosopher will not allow to read in the stars the reliability of astrology.... The problem is perhaps most acute if one thinks about first-person philosophical reflection about justification. If I really am interested in knowing whether astrological inference is legitimate,... I will not for a moment suppose that further use of astrology might help me to find the answer to my question.[16]

Fumerton is right to claim in this passage that there is a serious circularity in externalism if it is taken as an answer to the first-person question, but he is wrong in the last passage but one to read into externalism the idea that if externalism is true there is a perceptual route to its verification. There is nothing to guarantee, for externalists or anyone else, that if perception is a reliable process the perception of the reliability of perception is possible. Yet this is what Fumerton strangely claims. The most that externalism can say is that the fact that a perceptual state has been reliably produced or that perception is a reliable process is impersonally an answer to the sceptic. This fact counts against the sceptic in roughly the way that freedom from impurities like sulphur in the steel hull of a ship counts against a passenger's fear that an iceberg might pierce the hull. The passenger may not know how the hull of the ship is constituted, or know enough about steel or ship construction to make anything of the relative absence of sulphur content in the steel if he were made aware of it, but as a matter of natural law, the absence of that content makes the steel strong enough to resist penetration by icebergs and so answers his fear. In the same way, in some versions of externalism, the fact that a belief was produced by such and such a physiological process makes it likely, as a matter of natural law and independently of conscious reasoning on the subject's part, that a subject will believe a truth.

Now clearly scepticism is not answered impersonally – by how the facts are independent of the experience or beliefs of the subject. Scepticism has a point where, *relative to the subject's beliefs or what he could find out*, the subject has nothing to rule out the possibility of unreliably produced belief. And it is the resourcelessness of externalism when it comes to this first-person question that exposes it as inadequate. This is not a matter of circularity but of the independence from the first-person perspective of the facts that matter to adequate justification

[16] Ibid., p. 177.

or knowledge. To revert to Fumerton's formulation, it is not that the problem with externalism is at its most *acute* in the first-person case; it is that it begins and ends in the first-person case. Externalism has trouble with scepticism because it tries to bypass the first-person perspective.

Fumerton is nevertheless wrong to infer, in the last of the passages quoted, that if a concept needs extra-philosophical explication it is of no philosophical interest. This seems to me to imply that there can't be a philosophy of physics or mathematics because the concepts involved are drawn from outside philosophy and might require extra-philosophical knowledge to discuss. No one who doubts that externalism answers scepticism, or who thinks that the questions of traditional epistemology are not to be dismissed as incoherent, has to believe that philosophy is either aprioristic or that its conceptual resources and questions do not communicate with those of any other discipline that requires specialised extra-philosophical training. It is perfectly open to a philosopher, on account of the influence of extra-philosophical disciplines, to say that epistemology is too aprioristic, or to ask questions about knowledge in the light of cognitive psychology. The philosophical freedom to do this looks more limited to Fumerton than to me because he thinks that meta-epistemology is constrained to analyse concepts presupposed by normative epistemology.[17] If the price of a more inclusive reckoning of concepts of philosophical interest is the rejection of the meta-epistemology/normative epistemology framework, then let us reject the framework. Doing so need not make anyone suspect that scepticism is a philosophical pseudo-problem.

INTERNALISM AND THE ETHICS OF BELIEF

Externalism has trouble answering the sceptic partly because it does not acknowledge the need to answer the sceptic from the first-person perspective, and partly because it is indiscriminate about the pre-philosophical intuitions it should be deferring to while still contributing to epistemology. Internalism makes room for a first-person perspective and is better adapted to acknowledging the force of scepticism, but at the cost of implying that the difference between true belief

[17] Ibid., p. 2.

and knowledge is always a matter of something in or accessible to consciousness. Internalism is inadequate as an analysis of knowledge or justified belief in general, but it may fit the narrow and traditionally emphasised variety of knowledge or justified belief that depends on deciding what to believe. This is the area where Cartesian autonomy in knowledge also comes into its own, but it is not the whole of the area covered by the concept of knowledge or by the analysis of that concept.

We are in a position to decide what to believe when we are presented with evidence against something we believe and are *aware* that the evidence counts against that thing. People in the U.K. who voted Labour in 1997 may have believed that there would be a greater volume of public spending by the Labour government than was actually witnessed, and at a certain stage they may have dropped their expectation of greater public spending on the basis of contrary evidence. Whether they were right to do so depends on the strength of the evidence against the fulfilment of their expectation at the time the expectation was dropped. Prior to the election, however, voters may not have known what to believe. The question whether Labour would or would not raise public expenditure might have presented itself *then* as an open question. This open question might have subsequently given way to a belief in future, increased public spending as certain election promises were made. At first voters did not know what to believe, and then promises were used, perhaps properly, as the basis for a switch from the suspension of belief to belief. Both settling the open question and dropping a belief in the face of counter-evidence are cases of deciding what to believe by following the commonsense precept 'Proportion belief to the evidence'.

There are other commonsense precepts for deciding what to believe. In the case of belief based on testimony, it matters whether the informant has a history of truthfulness, or whether he might have an intention to mislead. To believe without taking these things into account can be a case of common or garden gullibility, and it can be criticised by pre-philosophical standards as easily as by the standards of an epistemology attuned to scepticism. Without assuming that compliance with precepts for deciding what to believe is a condition of *all* justified belief or knowledge, it seems reasonable to say that it is a condition of some knowledge or justified belief, namely knowledge or justified belief in cases where acquiring belief involves deciding what to believe. In these cases, the precepts are received and consciously acted upon in the first person, and so a kind of internalism also seems irresistible. This is not to say that a subliminal or subreflective sensitivity to evidence couldn't operate in pre-reflective beings or in reflective beings at certain times (as when something we can't quite identify makes us mistrust someone): It is only to say that, ordinarily and pre-philosophically, sensitivity to evidence *can* take the full-blown conscious form that is so familiar to us in life when we decide whether to believe an informant we don't know, or when we accept one rather than another plausible reading of certain evidence.

Internalism fits cases of deciding what to believe, but how many beliefs can result from such decisions? If Descartes is right, whole classes of beliefs can be suspended as 'prejudices' in the light of sceptical hypotheses and then made subject to decisions about their reinstatement. We earlier found reasons in Wittgenstein for finding the scope of belief subject to decision in this sense according to Descartes quite exaggerated. For example, we can neither seriously repudiate, nor afterwards decide to retain, the belief that every human being has parents, or that Earth has existed for many years. Perhaps the empirical facts about perception add to beliefs in this class. Perhaps if our sense-organs are normal and we have the relevant experience of red when seeing a pillar-box in normal conditions of illumination, we can't but believe that the pillar-box is red when we see it in normal conditions. Perhaps we can't help judging the lengths of the lines different in the Muller-Lyer illusion. Perhaps, in a different way, we cannot help believing that $2 + 2 = 4$ if we have any hold on the arithmetical operation of addition. Perhaps, in a different way again, we cannot help believing that, if anything is morally bad, sadistic torture is. The inalienability of certain beliefs seems to set limits to the capacity for deciding what to believe, and also to suggest cases of the directly evident. Again, they seem to be cases where one person's believing a thing is an expression in part of membership in a community. There seems to be a heterogeneous class of beliefs such that their being generally held explains any one person's holding it, rather than the belief's being generally held because lots of people arrive at it in their own separate ways. These beliefs, some of which may be drawn to our attention by externalism, strongly limit the scope of a credible internalism, just as they strongly limit the scope of a credible thesis of the autonomy of knowing.

Within the relevant limits, however, there is significant room for deciding what to believe. Such decision is not confined to the case of the open question and of conflicting evidence. There is also the case where there are alternatives to what subjects believe that are consistent with the subject's evidence but which are neither believed nor disbelieved, because they do not occur to the subject. In these cases it is not that the alternatives are unimaginable for the subject but that the subject has no special reason to consider them and rule them out where they conflict with what he does believe. For example, many people who can recognise my brother and hold perceptual beliefs about him are unaware that he has a twin, namely me. It never occurs to them that they might be misidentifying me as my brother, and because we live on different continents, its never occurring to them has no tendency to weaken the justification for the relevant beliefs. But my existence and whereabouts are relevant to the question of the reliability or justifiedness of their perceptual judgements. Other nonperceptual cases run along similar lines. When I read an excellent student essay, I sometimes wonder whether it has been plagiarised. But sometimes it doesn't occur to me – the style is what I would expect from a student, for example, or there are some incidental errors consistent with philosophical flair. Even when it doesn't occur to me, I could understand someone's raising the question of plagiarism, and if they were to do so, I might not be able to rule out the possibility. I might even begin to wonder whether the essay *was* plagiarised just because I had no reason to think it wasn't.

These small-scale counter-possibilities have something in common with sweeping sceptical counter-possibilities, for they are grounds for rational changes of mind or suspension of belief. On the other hand, they remind us that grounds for sceptical second thoughts can be pervasive without being general in content. Unlike the sweeping counter-possibilities, they can in principle be ruled out. My student's roommate can tell me about the long process of composition he went through, and the local shortage of reference sources on the student's subject. My brother's acquaintances can find out whether I was in my brother's vicinity when they saw somebody who looked like him. Given that the counter-possibilities can be ruled out, should they be? Is it up to everyone to rule them out or else suspend judgement? These questions belong to the normative ethics of belief that governs decisions what to believe. If the answer is 'Yes', it is possible to ask whether the ethics of belief is overdemanding – whether, for example, if its demands were met, the cost of trying to believe the true by ruling out counter-possibilities would lead to epidemic and insupportable indecision. Even if it is only for subjects to rule out those counter-possibilities that occur to them, it may seem as if subjects are being burdened with a scrupulosity about belief verging on paranoia. Once it is pointed out to them that my brother has a heretofore unsuspected twin visiting him, must my brother's acquaintances ask, with respect to everyone they can perceptually identify, whether *they* have twins in the vicinity, and suspend perceptual identification until they are sure the answer is 'No'? Whatever the right response, there is clearly a niche in epistemology for the question of what ethics of belief is demanding enough, but not overdemanding. Without supposing that all beliefs result from a decision what to believe or can be made the subject of such a decision *post facto*, we can suppose that an epistemology able to accommodate an ethics of belief will be, to that extent – and the extent is probably significant – internalist.[18]

INTERNALISM *AND* EXTERNALISM

One does not have to be Descartes or a practioner of meditative, methodological scepticism to believe that a first-person perspective is ineliminable in epistemology. One can believe in modest counter-possibilities and see the need for consciousness of these possibilities to be spoken to by an ethics of belief. In view of this, and the dangers of a purely internalist approach to the analysis of knowledge and justification, it may be prudent to aim at an analysis of knowledge that is a hybrid of internalism and externalism. This option and the reasons for finding it attractive have not gone unnoticed in the literature.

---

[18] For a much more thoroughgoing attachment to internalism, at least in the analysis of justified belief, see the third edition of R. Chisholm, *Theory of Knowledge* (Englewood Cliffs, N.J.: Prentice-Hall, 1989), ch. 8. Chisholm argues that externalist theories of justification are either empty – nontheories – or else have internalist elements.

William Alston has proposed a hybrid position,[19] and he has also given one of the most detailed surveys of the strengths and weaknesses of internalist theories of justification.[20] The strengths of internalism, according to Alston, lie in its fidelity to the practices of justification that give a theoretical interest in justification its point. We reflect critically on our own beliefs and wonder about the grounds for other people's, trying to elicit those grounds by asking other people to justify their beliefs. These practices help to establish a conceptual connection between a believer's being justified in holding a belief and the believer's having access to the justification.[21] Even where justification is identified in theory with believing in a such a way as to have a high chance of hitting the truth, if there is nothing to indicate *to* the believer that in believing a certain thing he *is* believing that way, then, according to Alston, to that extent the believer does not seem to have a justified belief after all. On the other hand, it is difficult to give conditions for access to grounds for belief that are not implausibly strong, or to give internalist conditions for having *good* grounds for belief that are not open to problems of regress.[22]

Alston's positive proposal combines an internalist account of what it is to have a ground for a belief with an externalist account of what it is for the ground to be adequate. To have a ground for a belief one must have undergone a process of belief-formation, such that whatever goes into forming the relevant belief is 'truth-conducive' – makes it probable that the belief will be true.[23] This truth-conducive content does not necessarily work by making the belief *seem* more probably true to the holder of it. It objectively probabilifies the belief. Truth-conduciveness is not tantamount to adequacy in a ground for belief: A belief can be grounded and yet not be well grounded or make the believer justified in holding it. In addition to being truth-conducive, the ground must be of a sort that one could normally come to be aware of 'fairly directly'. One need not be immediately conscious of one's grounds, and there

[19] 'An Internalist Externalism', reprinted in Alston's collection, *Epistemic Justification* (Ithaca, N.Y.: Cornell University Press, 1989), pp. 227–48.
[20] 'Internalism and Externalism in Epistemology', in *Epistemic Justification*, op. cit., pp. 185–226.
[21] 'An Internalist Externalism', loc.cit., p. 236.
[22] 'Internalism and Externalism', loc. cit., pp. 196–223.
[23] 'An Internalist Externalism', pp. 231–2.

could be a local explanation of why a particular believer with a ground for a certain belief was not able readily to come to recognise it on reflection. Still, a believer will have a ground in Alston's sense for believing something if the process of belief-formation is truth-conducive and most people with that sort of ground for belief could without too much trouble bring it to consciousness. These are the internalist components of Alston's account of justified belief. The externalist components constrain truth-conduciveness so that a ground, in addition to being of a type that tends to produce a true belief, is 'sufficiently indicative of the truth' of the particular proposition the ground is a ground for.[24]

Although I think there is much to commend Alston's account, his working out of it suffers from some of the same tacit assumptions about the strength and weakness of requirements of justification that earlier manifested themselves in our discussion of Goldman as a gratuitous or question-begging anti-scepticism. In Alston these tendencies are surprising, for he sometimes argues against certain approaches to the theory of justification – theories that confine justifiable beliefs to those that could be shown by their holders to be justified – on the ground that they narrow the scope of epistemically challengeable beliefs.[25] Yet when he considers and rejects one internalist condition of justification as too strong, he does so in ways that do seem to imply – question-beggingly – that we should tailor conditions of justification to what is normally and actually possible for the typical human being.

Alston discusses the following condition:

(II) S is justified in believing p only if S is capable, fairly readily on the basis of reflection, to acquire a justified belief that the ground for S's belief that p is an adequate one.

His objection is that, while (II) calls for something within human capacities, 'it is by no means always the case that the subject of a justified belief is capable of determining the adequacy of his ground, just by careful reflection on the matter, or, indeed, in any other way'.[26] On the contrary, according to Alston, most justified believers, even quite

[24] Ibid., p. 244.
[25] Ibid., pp. 235–6.
[26] Ibid., p. 240.

sophisticated ones, may not have the concept of adequate justification in the first place. So while they may have justified perceptual beliefs, for example, they may not have a ground for believing that they do, still less a ground for crediting themselves with adequate justification. Justified beliefs based on the authority of a source of information are another case in point:

> If we have been trained properly, we generally recognise the marks of compe-
> tence in an area, and when we believe the pronouncements of one who exhibits
> those marks, we are believing on adequate grounds, proceeding aright in our
> belief formation, and so [are] adequately justified. But how many of us can,
> on reflection, come up with adequate evidence on which to base the belief
> that a given putative authority is to be relied on? Very few of us.

This is supposed to be a conclusive argument against (II). Certainly it is conclusive if adequate justification is simply having a true belief whose ground objectively probabilifies the belief. But this condition might be met in the case that Alston and others think takes external-ism to extremes: the case of the person whose 'invariabl[y] correct beliefs about the future of the stock market come out of nowhere'[27] and are mysteriously true even to the subject. If there has to be some-thing from the point of view of the subject to count towards the truth of what he believes, then there has to be such a thing in the case of beliefs derived from perception or authoritative testimony. Now things satis-fying this condition are assumed to be present when Alston objects to (II). The person who is justified in believing something on the basis of perception believes because he sees, and his visual experience tells in favour of the truth of his belief. Similarly, the subject who believes on the basis of authoritative testimony has learnt the marks of the compe-tent authority, and it is the registration of those marks that produces belief. The fact that these marks or the role of the visual experience may not be able to be *called up* by the subject subsequently – *this* is the fact that Alston is saying takes nothing away intuitively from the status of the subject as being justified. But Alston has already embedded the source of requirements of justification in our practices of being able to reflect upon our beliefs and justify them to others: The perceivers and believers of authoritative testimony whom he is considering are

---

[27] Ibid., p. 235.

unable to go very far in either reflecting or justifying their beliefs to others. So they either lack something important in the way of justification, in which case (II) can be allowed to stand, or else they don't, and the stock market seer *is* justified in believing what he does, in which case externalist justification leaves nothing out after all.

I believe that the right way out of this dilemma is to say that our concept of justification does issue from the practices of critical reflection and meeting dialectical challenges *and* to admit that the norms of those practices make it a question far more often than we would like whether we or our beliefs meet them. This is why epistemological scepticism is not a world away from wondering in ordinary life whether we have reason to believe someone or whether we really did see that one in the identity parade rather than someone else entirely. The everyday doubts have a source in common with the more sweeping ones, namely that the grounds for our belief have gaps exposed by self-critical reflection or dialectical challenge. There is an upshot for Alston's claim that all that is required for a justified belief that p on ground G is that G be sufficiently indicative of the truth of p: The 'sufficiently indicative' condition cannot be satisfied entirely outside the access of the subject. Insisting on this is not to ask for the Cartesian autonomy of knowledge. Beliefs can be adequately justified and even knowledge-ranking without being *present* to the subject, without even being present under a description like 'thing I once proved I could be sure of if I could prove that God was no deceiver'. Autonomy of knowledge goes way beyond what the truth in internalism will deliver; but the truth in internalism is strongly anticipated in Cartesianism.

3

The Belief in Foundations

Enquiry has to start somewhere; but does that mean that there is a single preferred order of investigation, and that certain things have to be grasped before stable science of any kind is possible? Descartes's answer is 'Yes'. There *is* a preferred order, and a starting point in just a pair of propositions: 'I am thinking, therefore I exist'; and 'God exists and is no deceiver'. These were the supposed foundations of science in general, and had to be taken in before anyone could have a stable grasp of physics, medicine, mechanics, or morals. By 'stable grasp' Descartes meant a grasp that would not weaken in the face of the hypothesis that we might be constituted to find the false entirely certain. No one now thinks that science has the structure Descartes described, or that physics in particular, as we now have it, can be thrown into doubt by the absence of metaphysical first principles guaranteeing the trustworthiness of our cognitive faculties. Does this mean that foundationalism cannot be part of an innocent Cartesianism? It depends on whether the claim to have arrived at foundations has to be attended by a theory like Descartes's of the structure of science, and whether the effort of arriving at foundations makes sense only when there is general disbelief in the soundness of the results of a certain branch of enquiry, such as physics. It depends, too, on whether what is foundational has to *guide* enquiry.

In each of these cases, the answer appears to be 'No'. Foundational propositions may support science without entering the consciousness of scientists or guiding scientific enquiry. Again, there have been foundationalists who want no part of Descartes's picture of science as a tree whose roots are metaphysics, whose trunk is physics, and whose branches are medicine, mechanics, and morals. In particular, many twentieth-century foundationalists have denied that natural science, properly conducted, has to be informed by prior thoughts about the constitution of the human mind or God. What is more, foundationalism can make sense even when the reliability of physics is not in doubt. It can make sense for three reasons. First, it can strike us, as it struck Descartes, that being humanly constituted is not an asset for scientific understanding. On the contrary, it gets in the way, except as a source of scientific explananda. Our reliance on the senses, and the difficulty for most humans of acquiring the mathematical and other concepts required for natural science; the fact that human beings might not have evolved at all on Earth and that there could well have been no human science or much worse science – these facts call for an explanation of the success of natural science, even though its success is not in doubt. Few who believe in the predictive success of natural science and in its conceptual acuity are prepared to accept that its success is an accident. Some scientists like to trace its success to the content of theories and the experimental methods used to test them. Some *philosophers* of science like to trace the success of natural science not only to methods but also to necessities in nature or natural substances, which natural scientific theories somehow latch onto. Either way, the concern with foundations survives in proposals of a basis for the success of science.

The second way in which foundationalism makes sense is as a response to the idea that even the natural sciences are 'social constructions' that owe more of their success to human invention and convention than to truth, reference, objectivity, or the power of theories to track necessities in nature. Sometimes the idea that there is social construction in the natural sciences is allied to the idea that the natural sciences are *true* only relative to a relevant community or to humanity. It can contribute to showing that natural science is more than a social construction and more than relatively true to show that and how something outside the human mind or the human will makes it true or approximately true. Showing this contributes to providing philosophical foundations for natural science. There may even be a sense in which knowing that natural science is more than a social construction, and knowing how in general it has been successful at prediction, retrodiction, measurement, and control, is a condition of having a stable grasp of the individual sciences. Not to be sure how a natural science differs from a novel, a myth, or a religion can be a sign of an unacceptably unstable grasp of a natural science. So if Descartes is interpreted as saying that the identification of foundations makes a grasp of the sciences firmer, that may be right even if he *mis*identifies those foundations.

Finally, foundationalism makes sense against the background of the claims made in the previous chapter. I said there that there is such a thing as deciding what to believe. We arrive at some of our beliefs – in *and* out of science – on the basis of deliberating between alternatives we might accept as true. And we are guided by such precepts as that we should proportion belief to evidence or trust informants according as what they tell us coheres with well-established background information. How is it that these precepts can normally be relied upon? We know that 'evidence' can sometimes be manufactured, that our background beliefs can be altered by skilled confidence tricksters, by habit, by hypnotic suggestion and many other things. If the precepts for deciding what to believe work only in an environment free of such artifice, how do we know that the environment normally *is* free of such artifice, and why, in any case, should a 'natural' environment for belief-formation be favourable to forming true beliefs? Do we not have to fall back on some general assurance about the appropriateness of our capacities – perceptual, conceptual, and inferential – to the reality we perceive, and try to understand? The answer 'Yes' does not seem unreasonable. But it could have come straight out of Descartes.

In what follows, foundationalism will mainly be discussed in relation to the success of natural science and 'social construction' and as a response to relativism. In all of these areas, there is significant scope for innocent Cartesianism.

UNRECONSTRUCTED CARTESIANISM AND THE JUSTIFICATION OF THE NEW SCIENCE

Descartes helped to inaugurate the kind of natural science whose success now seems so familiar. But this science had inauspicious beginnings. Few of Descartes's contemporaries could have been confident that *any* genuine natural science – any systematic knowledge of the causes of observed facts – was humanly possible. Anomalies bedevilled traditional natural science, and the personal costs of proposing or endorsing a rival mechanical science were high. The new mechanical science in its turn was obscure in places. It sometimes invoked invisible internal structures of bodies to account for observed properties, and it seemed to endow inert matter with the power to act on minds. The *Essays* in the *Discourse* and *Essays* applied a version of the new mechanical science to problems that had defeated traditional natural science in optics and meteorology. A further *Essay* solved very longstanding problems in geometry. The *Discourse* indicated the 'method' that supposedly produced these results, and Descartes's message was that the same method might be applied to any number of further problems in the rest of the sciences.

Descartes, then, justified the new science at least twice. There is the nonmetaphysical justification offered in the *Discourse* and *Essays*. This justifies mechanical science by its results. Or, perhaps better, it justifies one kind of mechanical science by the problem-solving power of its general method. Then there is the metaphysical justification of the new science in the *Meditations*. I shall claim that both the metaphysical and nonmetaphysical justifications of science contribute important elements to a philosophically defensible foundationalism.

I start with the *Meditations*. It provides a proof, in the face of scepticism about all of learning, that *scientia* is possible for human beings (see esp. AT VII 69, 71; CSM II 48, 49). *Scientia* is a special kind of knowledge. It is systematic knowledge of a lot of related truths. So it contrasts with intuitions of single truths. Intuitions of single truths are knowledge; and so long as the attention is fixed, intuitions do not depend for their certainty on knowledge of God; but the attention naturally wanders, and the certainty of any one truth can be shaken by the principles for calling into question whole classes of belief that Descartes introduces in Meditation One (AT VII 18; CSM II 12). So intuition needs to be backed up by something that can overturn those principles: namely, the certainty that God exists and is no deceiver. *Scientia* is knowledge of a system of physico-mathematico truths that incorporates this assurance against general uncertainty.

And crucially, once it is arrived at, it is not open to reconsideration through doubt, not even through the doubt that our minds might be defective.[1]

Scientia is an unshakeable vision of a system of truth because it is a vision which includes *scientia* that God exists and is no deceiver. Being unshakeable and true, it resembles divine knowledge itself. God could not know now and later lose his knowledge, for he wills all that is eternally true all at once and for all time and cannot therefore fail to know what is willed to be true for all time. In other words, God's knowledge is unshakeable. Of course human *scientia* and divine *scientia* differ much more than they resemble each other. To the extent *we* have *scientia* it is by disciplining the attention, ordering its objects from simple to complex, and getting used to seeing totalities in the light of the simple. God's purchase on the objects of *scientia* is entirely different. For one thing, those objects are his creations, and he knows the natures of things by deciding what they will be, not by fixing his attention on them.

If God's immutability is both a model for human *scientia* and something we have to be aware of in order to acquire *scientia*, could not Descartes claim with justice to have made knowledge of God essential to the knowledge of nature, just as the theologians would have wanted him to do? The claim has some, but only some, plausibility in the context of the *Meditations*. But it is much weaker in connection with the *Discourse* and *Essays* and even weaker in his suppressed physics treatise, *Le Monde*. Let us stick to the *Discourse*. Not only does Descartes pass very quickly over metaphysical truths in Part Four, allowing the reader to infer from the brevity of his treatment that they do not matter much, but he also makes the very striking claim that the evident adequacy of the explanations of things in the *Optics* and the *Meteorology* is on its *own* a proof of the principles of Cartesian natural science put forward

---

[1] For more on the distinction between *scientia* and intuition (crucial to the issue over the Cartesian Circle) see A. Kenny, *Descartes: A Study of His Philosophy* (New York: Random House, 1968), ch. 8, and J. Tlumak, 'Certainty and Cartesian Method' in M. Hooker, ed., *Descartes: Critical and Interpretive Essays* (Baltimore, Md.: Johns Hopkins University Press, 1978), pp. 40–73. A more recent discussion is L. Loeb, 'The Cartesian Circle' in J. Cottingham, ed., *The Cambridge Companion to Descartes* (Cambridge: Cambridge University Press, 1992), pp. 200–35.

in at least the two first *Essays*. This is how we might understand the following famous passage from the end of the *Discourse*.

Should anyone be shocked at first by some of the statements I make at the beginning of the *Optics* and *Meteorology* because I call them 'suppositions' and do not seem to care about proving them, let him have the patience to read the whole book attentively, and I trust that he will be satisfied. For I take my reasonings to be so closely interconnected that just as the last are proved by the first, so the first are proved by the last, which are their effects. It must not be supposed that I am here committing the fallacy that the logicians call 'arguing in a circle'. For as experience makes most of these effects quite certain, the causes from which I deduce them serve not so much to prove them as to explain them; indeed, quite to the contrary, it is the causes which are proved by the effects. (AT VI 76; CSM I 150)

In the same vein, there is this passage from the letter to Mersenne of 27 May 1638:

You ask if I regard what I have written about refraction as a demonstration. I think it is, in so far as one can be given in a field without a previous demonstration of the principles of physics by metaphysics – which is something I hope to do some day but which has not yet been done – and so far as it has ever been possible to demonstrate the solution to any problem of mechanics, or optics, or astronomy, or anything else which is not pure geometry or arithmetic. But to require me to give geometrical demonstrations on a topic that depends on physics is to ask me to do the impossible. And if you will not call anything demonstrations except geometers' proofs, then you must say that Archimides never demonstrated anything in mechanics, or Vitellio in optics, or Ptolemy in astronomy. But of course nobody says this. In such matters people are satisfied if the authors' assumptions are not obviously contrary to experience and if their discussion is coherent and free from logical error, even though their assumptions may not be strictly true. I could demonstrate, for instance, that even the definition of the centre of gravity given by Archimedes is false, and that there is no such centre; and the other assumptions he makes elsewhere are not strictly true either.... but that is not a sufficient reason for rejecting the demonstrations.... (AT II 141–2; CSM III 103)

Demonstrations can be demonstrative, in other words, if they meet conditions far less exacting than those for metaphysical certainty. Or, in other words, there can be science without *scientia*.

Now it might be thought that whatever concessions are made to science lacking in metaphysical certainty in the *Discourse* and *Essays*, these concessions would be withdrawn in the *Meditations*. But this is not quite what one finds. If anyone lacks metaphysical certainty, according to the principles in the *Meditations*, it is someone who is ignorant of God's existence, or someone who denies it: an atheist. But does the atheist necessarily lack knowledge or science? More than one set of objectors to the *Meditations* thought this was implausible (cf. AT VII 124; CSM II 89; AT VII 414; CSM II 279), and the replies do not entirely disagree. Just as there can be a genuine demonstration that involves some incidental falsehood and that lacks metaphysical grounding, so there can be a kind of grasp of truth available even to those who think there is no God.

Descartes never even denied that in some sense of 'knowledge' the atheist could have knowledge; what he denied was that the atheist could have the preferred kind of knowledge called *scientia*:

> The fact that an atheist can be 'clearly aware that the three angles of a triangle are equal to two right angles' is something I do not dispute. But I maintain that this awareness of his is not true knowledge, since no act of awareness that can be rendered doubtful seems fit to be called knowledge. (AT VII 141; CSM II 101)

> As for the kind of knowledge possessed by the atheist, it is easy to demonstrate that it is not immutable and certain ... (AT VII 428; CSM II 289)

As if knowledge that was capable of being reconsidered critically could not *really* be knowledge. All we need interpret Descartes as saying, however, is that the atheist is bound to lack *scientia*. We do not need to interpret him as saying that *scientia* is the only knowledge there is. There is also a lesser, a non-ideal, kind of knowledge.

This category of non-ideal knowledge has an interesting range of application. Apart from the atheist's grasp of the property of the triangle, it extends to the grasp of a scientific truth by a scientifically open-minded believer who does not know Descartes's metaphysics, including churchmen who were instructed in optics and meteorology by the *Essays* and would have been instructed by *Le Monde* in physics, had it been released. More important, it applies to Descartes himself before he discovered his proofs of metaphysical truths in 1630. The fact that Descartes himself had only imperfect knowledge before 1630 may show that the scientific discoveries he made before 1630 were not *scientia* in the sense of the *Meditations*. But surely they counted as science. The fact that these discoveries might have been rendered doubtful or disputed by critics does not seem to make them count any less as science, just as the fact that the demonstrations of Archimedes might be corrected does not show that they were not demonstrations. On the contrary, it is the honorific sense of 'science' (science in the sense of *scientia*) and the honorific sense of 'demonstration' ('demonstration' in the sense of geometrical demonstration) that seems unduly narrow or stipulative – even, at times, from Descartes's own point of view as scientist. To some extent this narrowness is the result of grounding Cartesian science in the doctrine of God's nature.[2]

The point can be made in a different way that helps to introduce a parallel between the development of Descartes's views about the theoretical and practical sciences. Before 1630 – before science was metaphysically grounded – Descartes may be said to have developed a merely provisional philosophy of science broadly analogous to the *morale par provision* of the *Discourse*. The provisional philosophy of science is permissive about what to count as science. For example, it includes the imperfect demonstrations of Archimides and Ptolemy. Then there is the official or strict philosophy of science. This is the theologically correct one in which *scientia* is the human counterpart of divine knowledge. It excludes discoveries that can be rendered doubtful or that contain elements of falsehood, and it probably contains only the Cartesian sciences. The more restrictive philosophy of science is not necessarily a better or even more authentically Cartesian philosophy of science. Unshakeable certainty in physics or mathematics is intelligible as an ideal, of course, especially if divine *scientia* sets the pattern for human cognitive perfection. But openness to the opinions of others at least as intent as oneself on the truth is also consistent with a programme of enlarging knowledge. In the *Discourse* Descartes seems to have been keen to display such an open-mindedness, because

---

[2] It is true that in the passages just quoted, as at the very end of Meditation 5, Descartes is under the influence of the Platonic idea that while true beliefs can come and go, knowledge has got to be stable and fixed, tied down by the reasons for it. The idea is given a distinctively Cartesian gloss when stability is understood in terms of immutability of mind, and where the ideal mind is the immutable mind *par excellence* – God's. To the extent that Descartes's scientific practice requires a less metaphysically grounded philosophy of science than he constructed to please the theologians, to that extent, and I would say it is a considerable extent, Descartes can be said to have failed to make Cartesianism a better ally of Catholicism than Thomism.

he invited objections to his doctrines from his readers and promised to respond to them. This open-mindedness seems to have been more than a pose, moreover, as Descartes does seem to have seen the value of the work of his contemporaries – Harvey, for example, or Galileo, even Hobbes when it came to civil science. A different emphasis on unshakeable certainty, privately arrived at, seems to have started with the composition of the *Meditations*.

Both of Descartes's justifications of mechanical science – the metaphysical and the nonmetaphysical – contribute elements of enduring value to a philosophically defensible foundationalism. The nonmetaphysical account suggests that the more that a small number of conceptually uniform principles makes intelligible, the more they have a claim to be basic or foundational with respect to the chosen range of explananda. In this sense of 'foundation', it is a foundation of natural science that everything in nature is, or can be explained by, the variety of motions of material particles. To bear out this choice of foundation for natural science one does not necessarily have to recur to considerations outside natural science, according to the *Discourse*. It is enough that everything can be explained with a small number of principles, and that rival explanations are very much less economical and less *ad hoc*.

As for the metaphysical justification of natural science, it contributes the following to a philosophically defensible foundationalism: a conception of a method that makes science fruitful, and an explanation of that fruitfulness which depends on concepts and a mind that are not dependent on the senses. It is true that Descartes's use of God's mind as the prototype of a sense-independent human mind also brings with it the unwanted ideal of complete intellectual stability as the goal of enquiry. It is true, too, that the conception of the method that makes science fruitful is sometimes made to seem over-individualistic – a point I shall return to. But these unwanted elements are compensated for up to a point by the social character and open-mindedness of Descartes's scientific practice.

IDEAL METHOD AND ACTUAL PRACTICE

Descartes arrived at a range of pure mathematical and scientific results before he had articulated the method that supposedly led to them. The four precepts in Part Two of the *Discourse*[3] were probably written up *years* after some of the findings in the *Essays* on meteorology or the optics. So when he presents the method as having *led* to his meteorological and optical discoveries, that is a piece of autobiographical license. In addition, the precepts of the method underdetermine the results, and at times seem to conflict with the way that Descartes proceeds in the essays. Do they also contribute to the invention of a mythically rationalistic scientific method? A mythically individualistic method, perhaps. A method objectionably tied up to the ideal of the divinely unchanging mind, certainly. But not an inappropriately rationalistic method. Even if science in general, or Descartes's science, is influenced by forces that go well beyond rational ones – for example, a wish for fame, or an intention to carry out a divine mission revealed to Descartes in some dreams, or to act on a vision he experienced in a stove-heated room near Ulm, or to impress the Rosicrucians – Descartes's science and science in general are nevertheless to be judged, and judged primarily, by whether they give clear and convincing answers to factual questions, for example about the way clouds are formed or how the colours of the rainbow are produced, or, in the case of twenty-first-century science, whether the early universe experienced 'inflation'. In order to be convincing, the answers can be expected to be supported by reasoning, and to be nontrivially distinct from, and relevant to, what they explain. This is the blameless rationalism in Cartesianism about science.

I have spoken of reasons or reasoning 'supporting' Cartesian explanations, which in turn are relevant and distinct from what they explain.

---

[3] 'The first was never to accept anything as true if I did not have evident knowledge of its truth: that is, carefully to avoid precipitate conclusions and preconceptions, and to include nothing more in my judgements than what presented itself to my mind so clearly and distinctly that I had no occasion to doubt it.

The second, to divide each of the difficulties I examined into as many parts as possible, and as may be required to resolve them better.

The third, to direct my thoughts in an orderly manner, by beginning with the simplest almost easily known objects in order to ascend little by little, step by step, to knowledge of the most complex, and by supposing some order even among objects that have no natural order of precedence.

And the last, throughout to make enumerations so complete, and reviews so comprehensive, that I could be sure of leaving nothing out' (CSM I 120: AT VI 18–19).

At times, Descartes seems to make stronger claims about the way his explanations are related to the data:

Those long chains composed of very simple and easy reasonings, which geometers customarily use to arrive at their most difficult demonstrations, had given me occasion to suppose that all the things which can fall under human knowledge are interconnected in the same way. And I thought that, provided we refrain from accepting anything as true which is not, and always keep to the order required for deducing one thing from another, there can be nothing too remote to be reached in the end or too well hidden to be discovered. (CSM I 120; AT VI 19)

This passage has led some readers of the *Discourse* to think that for Descartes, natural scientific explanations are supposed to be laid out as formal geometers' proofs, and that they are supposed to reach conclusions as rigorously as in Euclid, and on the model of theorems being derived from axioms. We have already seen Descartes denying this. Far less than a mathematical demonstration suffices for demonstration in natural philosophy, according to him.

What geometry and the other natural sciences have in common is the order of moving from the maximally intelligible to the less intelligible by steps that are in turn intelligible and clear within the limits permitted by the subject matter under discussion. In the case of Descartes's own scientific essays, demonstration does not take the form of pages and pages of proof, but, typically, the elaboration of mechanical models of natural phenomena under investigation. Visible differences are like the differences in shape of tangible objects detected by a blind man's stick (CSM I 153; AT VI 85); the action of light on an illuminated object is like the action of wine in a full wine vat that can move towards either of two holes in the vat (CSM I 155; AT VI 87–8), and so on. If the models are oversimplified or inept in some other way, the explanation will fail. If, on the other hand, the model seems to capture the phenomenon under discussion, then the way the model works will illuminate (by indicating a possible way of working of) the phenomenon, too. The relation of the model and its workings to the phenomenon under explanation is not 'deductive' in any familiar, twenty-first-century, sense, but it *is* 'deductive' in *Descartes's* sense: a lot of different considerations are ordered from highly intelligible to less intelligible in a way that can be taken in by a continuous mental sweep free of doubt or unclarity. At the end of the deduction the less intelligible thing – for example, the action of light – is supposed to make sense against the background of the simpler considerations, including the way a mechanical model works.

Far from depending on long chains of reasoning or mathematical formulae, Cartesian explanations are often strikingly informal. If they convince, it is often through the perception of similarity between a mechanical model and a selected phenomenon, rather than through knock-down proof, or through the successful prediction of precisely measured effects from certain initial conditions.[4] Again, a Cartesian explanation purports only to find a possible cause of phenomena assumed to be producible in more than one way. So a Cartesian explanation does not claim that the phenomenon in question must have been produced in the way it describes, or that it could have been produced only that way. There are lots of ways in which an omnipotent God could have brought about any given effects (CSM I 144; AT VI 64–5). Descartes's method does require explanations or explanatory models to be at least as complex (to comprehend as many considerations) as the phenomenon under investigation or the problem to be solved. He does demand that the complex be understood in the light of the 'simple' or fundamental. And what is simple or fundamental relative to a problem or phenomenon in natural science is usually something to do with size, shape, position, path, or speed. But these conditions can be met and an explanation fall far short of being deductive or even conspicuously mathematical. When Cartesian explanations in natural science are convincing, then, that is not because they are compelling in the same way as geometrical proofs, or because they are special cases of mathematical proof.

The simples of natural scientific explanation were not the ultimate simples, and there were things – revealed by what is called 'philosophy' in the *Discourse*, or 'first philosophy' or 'metaphysics' in later

---

[4] For extended discussions of the difference between Descartes's official method and the scientific practice that is supposed to apply it, see Doren Recker, 'Mathematical Demonstration and Deduction in Descartes's Early Methodological and Scientific Writings', reprinted in T. Sorell, ed., *Descartes* (Aldershot: Ashgate, 1999), pp. 3–24, and, in the same volume, William R. Shea, 'Descartes: Methodological Ideal and Actual Procedure', pp. 25–37.

writings – that were simpler still and capable of illuminating the elements or simples of the natural sciences. The ultimate 'simple' is nothing other than God's nature, and we hit upon this by the methodological doubt that leads to the *cogito* and to reflection on the mind's ideas. It is the metaphysical application of the precept that the complex is to be understood in the light of the simple that yields the starting point of enquiry in general, as opposed to the starting point of any one science or any one solution of a scientific problem. Descartes sketches the path from this starting point to the elaboration of a complete natural science in Part Six of the *Discourse* (CSM I 143; AT VI 63–4). First he considers God's nature; then the heavens; then, on Earth, the elements and minerals. Then, on the basis of principles concerning these common and simple things, he arrives at hypotheses about more specific phenomena.

There is more than one reason why Descartes brings in the ultimate simples. He wants to appear theologically orthodox, and to embed his version of mechanical science in a metaphysics that supports theological orthodoxy. He wants to present the science he is proposing as systematic, rigorous, and general. He wants the explanatory shortcomings of the Aristotelian alternative to his own science to be connected with its reliance on the senses, and he wants to remind the theologian supporters of this Aristotelian science of its heathen origins. He wants to point out that the simples of natural science are just as sense-independent as the simples of metaphysics. Finally, and contrary to Aristotelianism, he wants to show that the simples of metaphysics belong to the same series as the simples of the natural sciences when the problem submitted to Descartes's method is the overarching one of how the whole range of scientific problems can be successfully solved by the human mind. Descartes brings in the most basic simples partly to show how science can be successful after a long run of failure in the hands of the Aristotelians. It can be successful – comprehend many observations with a small number of principles – when it is geared to the assumption that the most basic properties of the world are mechanical ones, and when ideas of those properties are assumed to be part of what we are endowed with by a benign, all-powerful God. In fewer words, the ultimate simples play an important role in a certain kind of success-of-science argument.

TWO KINDS OF SUCCESS-OF-SCIENCE ARGUMENT

Descartes's success-of-science argument is indirect, theological, and prospective. It succeeds if the hypotheses of the Dream and the demon deceiver can be overturned, and the theses are overturned if the mind can be shown to have within it the ideas of the mechanical properties of bodies even when doubt is taken to the limit. In this respect it is indirect. It is theological, in that God's existence and goodness underwrite the truth of mechanical explanations. It is not enough for truth that the explanations be couched in terms we find especially clear and compelling: The Dream and Demon call compellingness into question. Something further needs to assure us that what we find clear and compelling after careful reflection is true. Considerations about God and the soul are supposed to give us the required assurance. In Descartes's hands, they indicate that extension and motion are real properties of matter graspable by human beings, so that explanations in terms of extension and motion are not going to be empty. So much for the in-principle argument for the viability of science. The argument is prospective, in that Descartes assumes that mechanical science has no track record of success, and that it has never been elaborated as a complete science in a methodical way. The science whose success he wants to show is possible, the science small extracts of which are presented in the *Essays*, is largely a future science. It is not an already existing body of knowledge that is unknown to the general public, and that only needs publicity.

There is a tension between the strength of argument needed to overturn the Dream and Demon hypotheses, and the argument by results that one gets in the *Discourse* and *Essays*. Really to demonstrate the principles of metaphysics in a scepticism-proof way is a much taller order than to present a specimen of a natural scientific explanation that goes much further with less apparatus than an Aristotelian explanation. Or to put it another way, the refutation of philosophical scepticism is a taller order than that of dispelling scepticism about the possible success of any science, given the failures of Aristotelian science. The attempted refutation depends heavily on arguments about God's existence and nature that have never seemed compelling on their face to their readers, and that some have thought are circular or involve circular reasoning. Again, they may depend on assumptions that are illicit by the very high standards of the method of doubt. These problems do not show that there is no value in the Cartesian success-of-science argument. A version of it may come into its own when what is in question is not the viability in principle of natural science but the explanation of the success of natural science now that its success is beyond dispute. The issue now is not whether science can solve problems or answer questions at all but whether its ability to do so is deep and metaphysical or relatively shallow and sociological. If the reason science is predictively successful is to do with reference by our theories to independently existing things, or correspondence between theories and facts that independently obtain; if our ability to come up with such theories has to do with our having concepts that describe a deeper level of reality than that presented to our senses, then the explanation is deep and metaphysical. If, on the other hand, for example quarks are 'socially constructed',[5] or thyrotropin releasing factor is something that exists so long as a community of researchers does not call it into question,[6] then the success of science may be more sociological and more shallow.

One explanation of the progressive predictive success of science is that the entities it postulates, even the most recondite and hard to observe, really exist and have approximately the properties science ascribes to them. This is the realist explanation of the success of science, and it strikes some sociologists of science and some antirealist philosophers of science as objectionably metaphysical. Whatever else can be said against it, however, an explanation along these lines is incomplete. It raises the question of how we, or some experts among us, are able to discover highly recondite and hard-to-observe things, and also how we or the experts are able to tell apart these things from those postulated by now discredited theories of the elements of physical reality. Here descriptions in popular science of episodes of discovery are relevant. They often stress the unexpected observation or measurement. In the face of the unexpected, scientists do not typically respond by returning to first principles; they try to reinterpret or revise the relevant theory

[5] Andrew Pickering, *Constructing Quarks: A Sociological History of Particle Physics* (Edinburgh: Edinburgh University Press, 1984).
[6] B. Latour and S. Woolgar, *Laboratory Life: The Social Construction of Scientific Facts* (Beverly Hills, Calif.: Sage, 1979).

conservatively so that the unexpected and the previously correctly predicted phenomena are both predicted by a version of a working theory. Perhaps conceptual innovation will be necessary, or perhaps an already existing explanation of something else can be generalised.[7] Either way, the need to be consistent with what has already been observed and to preserve working theory and its correct results will heavily constrain any proposal, and the chance of the postulation of a perfectly fictitious element will be very small. In this way, the previous success of science vastly reduces the scope for the illusion of success later. Besides, the fact that in the physical sciences both observation and theory can be mathematically extremely exact makes explanatory success at a time, let alone over time, difficult to achieve.

Part of a retrospective success-of-science argument will be an account of how the revision of scientific theory proceeds. No doubt the explanation will partly be social. Theorists and experimentalists interact, and theorists and experimentalists compete with one another and also listen to one another's criticisms or ignore them. Certain journals are better respected and more widely read than others; findings or rival proposals in one are more likely to be given weight than those in another. Certain scientific conferences and networks are more prestigious and influential than others. A willingness to attend or belong may affect the character of scientific debate. And so on. These forces shape a theory and also explain how it is revised and turned into a more widely accepted theory, or else abandoned. But there will also be parts of an explanation of the success of science that will depend on the *content* of physical and mathematical theories *however* they have been arrived at, tested, and communicated, and the way that the content of a successor theory is more exact, or predictively more successful, or gets at truths more fundamental, than what it supersedes.

Here is where the explanation of success will appeal to something like 'simplicity' in Descartes's sense, as well as to truth, or to correspondence between the theory or ideas and reality. It will appeal for

---

[7] Another characteristic phenomenon is where theoretical calculations that are well motivated within a theory predict measurements that are known to be false. Then order needs to be restored. In particle physics, this can take the form of realising that the elements of a mathematical formula need systematic reinterpretation. See 'The Red Camaro' in Weinberg, *Facing Up: Science and Its Cultural Adversaries* (Cambridge, Mass.: Harvard University Press, 2001), p. 185.

example to the successor theory's finding more fundamental forces, fields, or particles than the predecessor theory, where 'more fundamental' corresponds to 'simpler' in Descartes's sense. And it will show that the successor theory corrects errors in predecessor theories. It will explain *how* the successor theory corrects errors, and why these were inevitable in the predecessor theory. The explanation of success may, unlike Descartes's, work with an evolving rather than a fixed picture of what the most simple is, and it may be more geared to increases in accuracy than to the truth of a theory once and for all. In this latter respect, it will part company with the far from innocent Cartesian idea that true science is finished and unrevisable. But it will keep faith with an idea that is as second nature to Descartes as to many scientific practitioners in our own day: that natural science is made true by, and is answerable to, a nature that is independent of natural science. Another Cartesian idea that fits in here is that nature is very superficially revealed in sense-experience and its deeper levels are available only to a mind using concepts – mathematical ones, for example – that do not derive from the senses. These ideas can be regarded as enduring Cartesian ideas in a pro-science philosophy of science, as well as in the prephilosophical understanding of mainstream scientists themselves.

What about the Cartesian foundational idea that only the nature of God gives us adequate assurance that our capacities are equal to the demands of science? A *retrospective* success-of-science argument, such as we are considering, may make redundant any large-scale in principle guarantee that we have the capacities to arrive at successful science. The explanandum of a retrospective explanation of the success of science takes success as given. Human beings *can* succeed at science because they have. But the fact of success had better not seem to be a miracle. It has to be made sense of by *how* it has been achieved. How scientists have proceeded – as revealed by the history of science – had better be reasonably rational, or else the connection between what makes the theories true and how they have come to be formulated and accepted will be obscure, and the success of science will look like an accident. This gives the history of science an important role in determining whether rationality makes an important contribution to the success of science.

Consider three possibilities. First, scientific practice is revealed by the history of science to obey a strict and substantial method of enquiry, as in the idealised story told in the *Discourse*; second, scientific practice is seen to be unmethodical, perhaps not really a case of enquiry at all[8]; or, third, scientific practice is rational by a measure that is messier than strict conformity to the precepts of a method. Probably none of these possibilities captures all practice throughout the recognised natural sciences; and probably not even the physical sciences are covered by the first. But the second possibility has been given wider currency than it deserves by sociologists of science who attempt to reduce recognition of evidence for and against a theory to a species of political negotiation between members of a research community. The fact that the sociological descriptions are straightforwardly challengeable, and leave plenty of room for the third of our possibilities, is an important source of support for a picture of the rationality of science less idealised than Descartes's but still rationalist.[9]

DESCARTES'S FOUNDATIONS AND INNOCENT CARTESIAN FOUNDATIONS

All of the following might be regarded as foundations of natural science in an innocent Cartesian foundationalism – one that explains the success of science. There are truths more fundamental than those able to be grasped on the basis of senses; these more fundamental truths stand to the less fundamental in more or less the way

---

[8] Not just any practice can count as enquiry. Its truth-seeking character is distinctive. See Susan Haack, 'Concern for truth: what it is and why it matters' in P. Gross, N. Levitt, and W. Martin, eds., *The Flight from Science and Reason* (New York: N.Y. Academy of Sciences, 1996), pp. 57–63.

[9] The work of challenging social constructivist accounts of science is well advanced. See James Brown's excellent *Smoke and Mirrors: How Science Reflects Reality* (London: Routledge, 1994), esp. ch. 3 on Latour and thyrotropin releasing factor. See also, on the alleged social construction of quarks, Weinberg, *Facing Up*, op.cit., pp. 266–7. For an open-minded consideration of social constructivism as one among many anti-science movements, see Gerald Holton, 'The Anti-Science Phenomenon' in his *Science and Anti-Science* (Cambridge, Mass.: Harvard University Press, 1993), esp. pp. 153ff. For a much more hostile but still persuasive treatment of an even wider range of anti-science phenomena, see M. Bunge, 'In Praise of Intolerance of Charlatanism in Academia' in Gross, Levitt, and Martin, eds., op.cit., pp. 96–115. A more moderate critic of social constructivist accounts of science is Ian Hacking, *The Social Construction of What?* (Cambridge, Mass.: Harvard University Press, 1999), ch. 3. Hacking discusses Weinberg's anti-constructivist views. For Weinberg's response, see *Facing Up*, op.cit., ch.23.

that Descartes's 'simples' stand to what Descartes called 'complex' problems and phenomena. Some of the more fundamental truths in the case of natural sciences are mathematical. These are principles for explaining observations. Mathematics also has its own principles and consequences of principles that are not explanatory of observations but that can be ordered as fundamental and derivative. There are further truths – this time from metaphysics – which say that the simple truths explain the complex ones because the world that exists independently of the senses contains natures corresponding to or referred to by the simple truths. This is as true in pure mathematics as in mixed (i.e., applied) mathematics. What is more, human minds are able to acquire concepts that are needed to express the more fundamental truths.

Although all of this is strongly reminiscent of Descartes, it omits any mention of God and makes no room for the *cogito*. The *cogito* is made redundant partly because I have associated innocent Cartesian foundations with an explanation of the success of science, and not a proof of the possibility of science in the fact of radical scepticism. It is meeting the demands of radical scepticism that gives a role to the *cogito*. The question is whether there is anything one can be certain of when there is no guarantee against deception, and the answer is that there *is* – one's own existence, given consciousness. But this much gives no insight into the natures of things, not even the nature of the self. It produces a certainty about existence only. Knowledge of natures starts to be reconstructed in the *Meditations* only after the *cogito*. And stable knowledge of natures starts to be reacquired by the 'I' of the *Meditations* only after God's existence is proved. So even in the proof of the possibility of science in the face of scepticism, the *cogito* is foundational only in the sense of being a first discoverable but unshakeable truth, not in the sense of being a first truth about the nature of anything. The first truth about the nature of a thing is the second of Descartes's first principles: the principle that an undeceiving God exists. This is foundational both in having to be arrived at before there can be knowledge that *scientia* is possible for human beings *and* in laying down a first item of *scientia*. The foundational status of the *cogito* is weaker.[10]

---

[10] This point is a commonplace in French commentary on Descartes and has been well known since 1953, when Gueroult discussed the different orders of reasoning in the Meditations. For an interpretation of its general significance, see P. Ricoueur, 'The Crisis of the *Cogito*', *Synthese* 106, pp. 57–66.

It is weaker still if the proof of the possibility of science is replaced as the context for foundationalism by an explanation of the success of science.

What about the second of Descartes's first principles? It has a presence in the foundations proposed by innocent Cartesianism, though not in its original form. The second principle is that God exists and is no deceiver. The nondeceivingness of God plays a complicated role in the argument of the *Meditations*. It is the special case of God's benevolence that is relevant to the epistemological concerns of the book. It consists not only of God's not playing the role of the demon in Meditation One but also of his constituting us to be able to penetrate to the natures of things, and constituting us to be able to be sure that we are able to. God's nondeceivingness is what is supposed to settle once and for all – beyond the occasions when we are having particular clear and distinct ideas – that clear and distinct ideas are true. In particular, it is supposed to assure us that the clear and distinct ideas of God's nature, the nature of bodies, the nature of minds, and mathematical natures are true. But God's nondeceivingness is also supposed to signal the possibility of a fit between what is deeply true of things and what creatures with minds like ours are able to intuit and arrive at by inference. This possibility of fit is what innocent Cartesianism takes over from unreconstructed Cartesianism. Although the natures of things are not presented to us on a plate, although we have to work them out, and although this working out is impossible for us without a method that is not innate, we *can* work them out, and we can work out, too, that there is no defect in us that prevents us from working them out. Or, to put it in the terms of Meditation One, we can be sure despite the Dream argument and despite the Demon argument that the most simple and universal things embedded in our ideas are real, and that these are the starting points of *scientia*. This is the counterpart, in the foundations of science proposed by *innocent* Cartesianism, of the thought that the simple truths explain the complex ones because the world that exists independently of the senses contains natures corresponding to or referred to by the simple truths.

Now God has other properties than nondeceivingness that are important to the argument of the *Meditations* and that will turn out to be important to innocent Cartesianism as well. There is the property of omnipotence, and in particular the ability to produce as separate whatever we can carefully distinguish in thought, and to put together or not what to us seems, even on reflection, to be necessarily and eternally united. Apparent necessities are in fact contingent because they are created by a God who was free not to have created them, but who, having created them, would not take them apart. And other composites that need not go together – our nature and existence; the nature of the human mind and the nature of the human body; motion and extension; the instantiation in matter of mathematical natures that can exist on their own – exist as composites because God wills that they should. A way of summarising what Descartes does with omnipotence is by saying that he invokes it to make sense of a *single* reality that contains a lot of different natures, and to unify contingent and necessary combinations of these natures. The different natures occupy a single reality – that is, the product of God's will. Natures that need not exist together do so because God wills it – the same reason that necessary combinations exist.

Innocent Cartesianism, too, needs the idea of a single reality containing at least mathematical, psychological, and material things, and to the extent that this idea is suggested by God, it is open to such an idea. But, as will emerge (Chapter 4), innocent Cartesianism is also able to say that it is (so far, at least) a mystery how mathematical, psychological, and material reality belong to a single reality.

ANOTHER INNOCENT CARTESIANISM ABOUT FOUNDATIONS?

I have been interpreting unreconstructed Cartesian foundationalism as belonging to a proof of the possibility of natural science. I have been sketching an innocent Cartesianism about foundations as making sense within a project of explaining the undisputed success of natural science. But mine is not the only possible idea of an innocent Cartesian foundationalism. Thomas Nagel takes himself to be following a Cartesian foundationalist strategy in *The Last Word*.[11] He attacks varieties of late-twentieth-century and early-twenty-first-century academic subjectivism by showing that one has to be objectivist – believe

---

[11] (Oxford: Oxford University Press, 1997).

that some truths are true full stop and some reasoning sound full stop – even to try to reveal objectivism as an *illusion*. And he takes the in- evitability of objectivism about certain forms of thought to be one of the things Descartes is trying to establish in the *Meditations*.

He associates Descartes with a project of asserting the authority of reason, where reason, as Nagel conceives it, provides regulative meth- ods and principles applicable to a raw material of perception and intuition, both about how things are and how to act.[12] And he takes himself to be following Descartes in trying to defend reason, so con- ceived, against those who think either that there is no such thing, or that whatever counts as reason does not endow conclusions reached rationally with the kind of authority they are supposed to have. Nagel thinks of the methods and results of reason both to have a kind of universality – to apply across cultures, species, and the like, and some- times to be true of huge totalities of things. He also thinks that the regulative principles he associates with reason are hard or impossible to think of as overridable.[13]

Although I am entirely in sympathy with this rationalistic project and do not deny that at least some of it deserves to be called Cartesian, I think it is neither entirely innocent nor really a kind of foundation- alism. On the one hand, too *many* kinds of thought turn out to be foundational for Nagel, and, on the other hand, the reasons why they are foundational turn out to be too varied to put it beyond doubt that a *unitary* reason – both practical and theoretical – is authori- tative. The reason that Descartes himself tries to show is authorita- tive is more unitary than Nagel's, but its authority may not rub off in quite the way one would like, if one is a rationalist, on practical reason.

A good place to begin is with Nagel's take on the *cogito*:

It reveals a limit to the kind of self-criticism that begins when one looks at oneself from the outside and considers the ways in which one's convictions might have been produced by causes which fail to justify or validate them. What is revealed in this process of progressively destructive criticism is the unavoidability of reliance on a faculty that generates and understands all the sceptical possibilities. Epistemololgical skepticism . . . proceeds by the rational

[12] Ibid., p. 16.
[13] Ibid., pp. 14ff.

identification of logical possibilities compatible with the evidence, between which reason does not permit us to choose. In the *cogito* the reliance on reason is made explicit, revealing a limit to this type of doubt. The true philosophical point consists not in Descartes' conclusion that he exists (a result more limited than he subsequently relies on), nor even the discovery of something absolutely certain. Rather, the point is that Descartes reveals that there are some thoughts one cannot get *outside of*.[14]

In the case of the *cogito* there is no means of criticising it from within the reasoning that is used to generate the sceptical possibilities. But it turns out that the *cogito* is not unique. The attempt at rational criticism in other domains leaves a residue of thoughts that cannot be criticised in those domains either:

Logic cannot be displaced by anthropology. Arithmetic cannot be displaced by sociology, or by biology. Neither can ethics, in my view. I believe that once the category of thoughts that we cannot get outside of is recognised, the range of examples turns out to be quite wide.[15]

But this poses a problem. What is the relation between a thought that one cannot get outside of in ethics and a thought one cannot get outside of in logic? What is the relation between either of these thoughts and the *cogito*? If there is no relation except that of being inescapable or of bringing a relevant line of rational criticism to an end, are all of these thoughts on a level?

Yes and no. Nagel has just been quoted as saying that they all belong to a single category. On the other hand, it is important to his argument against subjectivism that there are truths – mainly physical, mathematical, and logical – more basic than the social, historical, and psychological truths that subjectivism uses to expose things as constructions or projections. In Nagel's terminology, logical, mathematical, and physical truths *dominate* psychological, social, and historical truths.[16] Nagel's belief in a hierarchy of truths, recognizably Cartesian, is sometimes obscured by his idea that truths of *all* kinds are criticizable only within limits. According to Nagel, all kinds whatever of subjectivist criticism of ideas with objectivist or universalistic pretensions are for all that *criticism* – and criticism inevitably involves an investment in some

---

[14] Ibid., p. 19.
[15] Ibid., p. 21.
[16] Ibid., p. 64.

rational standards or other that hold beyond the matter at issue, as well as a subject matter that outruns the content of the criticism. But the idea that mathematical and physical truths *in particular* are presupposed by psychological and political explanation, and that they are *distinctively* hard to deflate as products of psychology and politics, is clearly important in the onslaught against subjectivism at its most general. If mathematics and physics are not open to any sort of convincing subjectivist reinterpretation, then subjectivism starts to be initially plausible only for some subject matters. Even where it *is* initially plausible – in some disputes about value, for example – it may not be tenable on reflection. But if in certain cases it seems out of the question, a kind of bedrock is reached.

Take a common subjectivising strategy that might be tried on '2 + 2 = 4'. It is sometimes thought to undo the compellingness of the simplest mathematical truths to reflect that they are arrived at by creatures whose existence is a sort of cosmic accident and who are highly adapted to the peculiarities of life on this planet, so that there must be something parochial about even the most elementary truths of a mathematics devised by humans. But to get this far, we need to be able to place ourselves in a cosmic evolutionary story that depends for its truth on the truth of at any rate some mathematical thoughts, for example thoughts leading to estimates of how long conscious life has existed on Earth. Because it is a partly mathematical ladder that we are using to climb out of our compulsion not to question mathematics, the ladder does not really help us to escape.

Nagel indeed goes further to say, in the case of the rules of inference of logic and the elementary truths of arithmetic, that they are part of the bedrock in the sense that there is no alternative to them.[17] Everything we think must be consistent with them, and any attempt to try to question them is bound to fail. It is bound to fail not on account of the personal limitations of the questioners, but on account of the concepts with which we would do the questioning, concepts that do not permit the questions to be raised in the first place. Here Nagel breaks from Descartes, for he thinks (correctly, in my view) that not even a malicious demon or God could make it even seem true that 2 + 2 = 5. The

---

[17] Ibid., p. 69.

concepts of addition and of the numbers involved do not permit it.[18] And while conceptual change is possible, and theoretical innovation can supply concepts where previously there was a void and the mere impression of inconceivability,[19] only by developing the concepts can the conceivability be created. In the case of arithmetical and logical truths, the attempt to conceive of a possibility that would undermine them or supersede them has to be self-defeating: For anything to be undermined by reason, logical truths (such as '-[A & -A]') must hold, or else the counterpossibilities run on hypotheses – 'If my brains were scrambled' – that undermine even those hypotheses.[20] Another way of putting some of what Nagel has in mind is that logical and mathematical propositions are strongly impersonal in content. They are not about me or my community even though they can be thought by me and my community, and so no account about the contingency of my existence or my community's or of the existence of my thoughts can exhaust its content or call its content into question.

Empirical science does not have a mind-independent subject matter in quite the same sense as mathematics, but the natural world – the universe – *is* unimaginably big and long-lived, relative to our spatio-temporal history even as a species, and some hypotheses cover its entire history or spatial extent or both. They are not just views of how things perceptible from Earth are in the twenty-first century, but views about how the universe as a whole has developed that are supposed to hold good regardless of where its authors come from, what species they belong to, or the date on which they were devised. The hypotheses may be wrong, but even to be wrong there must be some way the (whole) universe is that the hypotheses fail to capture, and this idea of there being a way the world is anyway may be a fixture of reason – something to which there is no alternative.[21] This is the idea that eludes an 'external view' of scientific understanding, one that attempts to reduce what is physically true to what we need to posit for example to 'cope' with nature or survive to reproduce our kind in it. Even if

---

[18] Ibid., pp. 59ff.
[19] Ibid., p. 65.
[20] Ibid., p. 62: 'I can't regard it as a possibility that my brains are scrambled, because I can't regard it as a possibility that I'm not thinking. Nor can I appeal to the possibility of a gap, in a case as simple as this, between what I can't think and what can't be true.'
[21] Ibid., p. 81.

one can get outside thoughts about the whole universe, the standpoint that one retreats to cannot be that of evolutionary theory, because it presupposes physics – for example, as an account of what there was before biological evolution started. Nor can it be that of psychology, for that is dependent for its truth on physics. Nor history, for the same reason.

There is not only a category of, but a hierarchy among, the thoughts that one cannot get outside of, at any rate in the sphere of application of theoretical reason. According to Nagel, logic dominates mathematics,[22] which dominates physics, and each and all of these dominate biology, anthropology, and history. This raises the question of what is supposed to be foundational in Nagel's variation on the Cartesian theme. Is it, as he sometimes implies, the forms of thought one cannot get outside or to which there is no alternative? Or is it, as his insistence on the priority of logic implies, the most fundamental truths of, or patterns of reasoning of, logic? And where, in all of this, does the *cogito* fit? It is neither a logical, mathematical, nor empirical scientific truth. So how is it to be related to Nagel's hierarchy of truths? Again, is the *cogito* a thought it is impossible to get outside of on its own, or only as the end point of a process of trying to doubt everything? I do not think any of these questions gets a clear answer in *The Last Word.* This is because Nagel's enterprise is less clearly defined than Descartes's, and probably quite different even though it shares with Descartes's a commitment to the authority of reason.

One way in which it is different also reveals a way in which it is controversial, and more controversial than a Cartesian belief in foundations has to be. The difference I have in mind is that in Nagel, but not in Descartes, what is attempted is a defence of reason – theoretical *and* practical, against subjectivism. Nagel thinks of this as a unitary project because he thinks that both practical and theoretical reason are concerned with justification and with articulating propositions whose content is universal in appropriate ways. In the case of the theoretical sciences, subjectivism is usually antirationalist or irrationalist, concerned to question or deny the authority of reason. But in the case of practical reason it need not be, and often is not. There *are* subjectivist attacks on ethics that also try to show that we shouldn't do what it

---

[22] 'Simple logical thoughts dominate all others, and are dominated by none' (p. 64).

asks. For example, there is the thought – discernible in some form in
Nietzsche – that orthodox ethics has no authority because it masks what
can be recognised as small-minded impulses, like resentment, envy,
cowardice, and so on. This *does* attack ethics by trying to see through
the reasons it gives for its precepts. But sometimes subjectivism will be
trying only to find bases for people's action that do not presuppose
access to special kinds of reality or special kinds of intellectual insight.
The Platonism of some ethical theories rather than their precepts can
be what is at issue.[23] Here, as Nagel concedes, a subjectivist position has
nothing to do with the aim of debunking ethics. He admits that in the
case of practical reason, subjectivism can sometimes consist not in an
attack on reason – in a kind of irrationalism – but as an attempt to show
that the apparent authority of certain precepts is due not to their justification but to a certain psychological or sentimental uniformity in
human beings combined with the appropriate stimuli. This kind of
subjectivism is not an attack on the authority of reason, or an attack
on the authority of ethics, but rather an attempt to show that the authority of ethics is due to something other than reason, and that things
other than reason can lie behind a respectable ethics. The appropriate response to this is not properly called rationalist, as if what was at
stake was the rationality of ethics; instead it is antireductionist. Not
everything that seems to be justificatory in ethics can be reconstructed
as complicated sentimental reaction, widely shared.

Descartes is a rationalist in ethics, but he always regarded ethics as
a highly derivative science, partly because he thought that what was
worthwhile to do in life depended on *scientia* about the perfections of
mind and body (metaphysics) and *scientia* about the workings of the
human body (physics). This view does not imply that practical reason
is a species of theoretical reason or that ethics is an explanatory science
rather than one that motivates with authoritative reasoning of its own.
It does not imply that people cannot disagree morally. But Descartes
does not attempt a defence of practical reasoning as he attempts a defence of theoretical reasoning. Rationalism in his book is the attempt
to show that and how agents can be moved by things other than unwilled appetites and aversions, as well as an argument that it is better

---

[23] This is what motivates Mackie's subjectivist argument from queerness. *Ethics: Inventing
Right and Wrong* (Harmondsworth: Penguin, 1976).

4

Conscious Experience and the Mind

The hallmark of innocent Cartesianism in the philosophy of mind is the claim that consciousness is irreducible. There have been intimations of this sort of view for a long time. In the early 1970s, Kripke was insisting that pain couldn't but be conscious and so couldn't be identical with C-fibre firing if, as he claimed it might, C-fibre firing could occur unconsciously.[1] At about the same time, Nagel was pointing out that there is irreducibly something it is like to be in certain psychological states, and that this is what makes the mind–body problem intractable.[2] Others, including John Searle,[3] Colin McGinn,[4] and Galen Strawson,[5] have more recently said similar things. To the extent that these claims remain defensible, Cartesianism in the philosophy of mind is a live and respectable option.[6]

---

[1] 'Naming and Necessity' (Oxford: Blackwell, 1984), pp. 144ff. Kripke's intuitions have been questioned by Shoemaker. See *The First Person* (Cambridge: Cambridge University Press, 1996), pp. 16off.

[2] 'What is it like to be a Bat?' *Philosophical Review* 1974. Reprinted in *Mortal Questions* (Cambridge: Cambridge University Press, 1979), pp. 165–80.

[3] *The Rediscovery of the Mind* (Cambridge, Mass.: MIT Press, 1992).

[4] *The Problem of Consciousness* (Oxford: Blackwell, 1991) and *The Mysterious Flame* (New York: Basic Books, 1999).

[5] *Mental Reality* (Cambridge, Mass.: MIT Press, 1994).

[6] Another approach is represented by John Foster's *The Immaterial Self* (London: Routledge, 1991). This is more self-consciously Cartesian than the others, and defends the idea of an immaterial subject. It is also unusual in being put forward alongside a rarely defended phenomenalism (p. 12). I think both phenomenalism and the idea of an immaterial subject are philosophically unattractive, that the former is not even

I shall begin by outlining unreconstructed Cartesianism about the mind and shall try to extract from that the elements of the corresponding innocent Cartesianism. Turning to signs of that latter position in the current philosophy of mind, I shall consider briefly what Galen Strawson calls 'naturalised Cartesianism'. Although I am sympathetic to Strawson's view, I do not want to endorse it in its entirety: There is a strong – and defensible – *anti*-naturalism in Descartes's philosophy of mind, and perhaps that deserves to be preserved in an innocent but latter-day Cartesian position. A similar thought is prompted by other writings from the twentieth-century philosophy of mind, notably McGinn on consciousness. Even in writers who do not belong to the mainstream, such as Strawson and McGinn, there is excessive deference to naturalism. The limits of naturalism are just as much at issue as the nature of the union between mind and body, if there is no clear naturalistic account of that union. At the end of the chapter, I consider what might be said by critics of even a sanitized position derived from Descartes. Much of the critics' rhetoric depends on suspect analogies or rebuttable claims about the unwanted consequences of *any* Cartesian position.

DESCARTES'S SOUL AND UNRECONSTRUCTED CARTESIANISM ABOUT THE MIND

Descartes and Cartesianism are reviled by virtually all of those in the twenty-first-century philosophy of mind who think that mental states can be reduced without remainder to brain states. So it is ironic that the view of mind put forward by the historical Descartes was itself part of a reductionist drive – against the traditional explanation of the vital functions in human beings. Far from finding excuses to cite the soul or soul-like entities or the soul's capacities in the explanation of human or animal functioning, Descartes explicitly insisted that they should be invoked only when there was no alternative. He rejected the Aristotelian idea that a special vegetative soul or vegetative capacities of sensitive or rational souls had to be posited to explain digestion, procreation, growth, sensation, and locomotion; according to him,

Cartesian, and the latter does not square with what Descartes says about embodiment. Foster's claims, then, seem to me to be neither innocent nor Cartesian.

these and many other functions (the circulation of blood, for example) could be explained with the very same mechanical apparatus – one that mentions only sizes, shapes, and speeds of material bodies – that he used to explain the behaviour of inanimate bodies in nature, or the behaviour of automata. What the rational soul *had* to be invoked to explain, Descartes said in Part Five of the *Discourse on the Method,* was the (as Descartes thought) uniquely human ability to use language appropriately, and to adapt spontaneously to different situations, without having to have a special disposition implanted for any particular sort of behavioural routine.[7]

Things that could take place unthinkingly, like the healing of a wound, no more needed to be attributed to the operations of a soul when they occurred in human behaviour than when they occurred in the behaviour of a cat or dog. But the ability of virtually all people to conduct a conversation derives from human reason, according to Descartes, and no animal faculty could naturally account for it. When Descartes explains why he reserves the rational soul for the explanation of that sort of human behaviour, he does not say that animals are *incapable* of speech, or *incapable* of adapting as necessary to changing circumstances: He says that as a matter of fact they do not display either behaviour to the degree that makes it compulsory to invoke a special explanatory principle to account for it.[8] And as it is only to encompass otherwise unencompassed behaviour that Descartes multiplies explanatory principles, he is not methodologically out of line with those who think that physics explains practically everything, and that one needs a reason to depart from a physical explanation even of the behaviour of humans.

Some of this is obscure to philosophers of mind in our own day, because they know Descartes's views on the soul only from the *Meditations,* where its role in the explanation of behaviour is eclipsed by two other roles: (i) as an ineliminable, apparently self-subsistent, and utterly certain object of introspection; and (ii) as the subject of doubt and demonic deception. In neither role does the soul get invoked to explain any human behaviour. Nor does it, in these roles, need to be

---

[7] CSM I 139–40; AT VI 55–9.
[8] He does say that it is inconceivable a machine could display a linguistic ability comparable to that of humans (CSM I 140; AT VI 56–7).

conceptualised as the soul, according to Descartes. What performs roles (i) and (ii) is the self or the 'I', which is supposed to be partially intelligible to us before we know what kind of thing – a mind, a rational animal, a body, or a soul – the 'I' is. The self of metaphysics connects up with the soul of Descartes's physiological writings by way of three things: first, the metaphysical claim that thought alone is essential to being a mind; second, the partly definitional thesis that thought is always present or accessible to consciousness; and third, the observationally supported claim that some of the processes attending human sensation, nutrition, locomotion, and bodily damage, even existence within the womb, are 'thinking' processes occasioned by mechanical processes that involve the vital organs and the brain.

Well-known problems attend Descartes's understanding of 'thinking' processes, and the nature of the interaction between Cartesian thinking and bodily processes is famously obscure. There are well-known problems associated as well with the claim in the *Meditations* that the mental and the physical have natures that are entirely separately graspable. If functionalism is correct, then the nature of mental states is given by their causal role, which cannot be specified without reference to physical behaviour and physical stimuli. Even if functionalism is false, it is hard to believe that the nature of the mental is exhausted by the concept of thought, at any rate the unreconstructed Cartesian concept of thought. Descartes's insistence on a nature for the mental entirely separate from the nature of matter even seems inconsistent with his interactionism, for how can thought affect or be affected by bodies without having to be capacities for motion and position only bodies are supposed to have? And it is odd to assimilate the awareness of bodily motion or pain to 'thinking'.

Some of the tensions in the account are explicable and excusable, given the highly ambitious way in which Descartes sought to combine metaphysics with natural philosophy. In the progress from the natural philosophy of the *Treatise on Man* to the metaphysics of the *Meditations*, Descartes tried to collapse the distinctions between the vegetative soul of human physiology and biology, the immortal soul of Catholic doctrine, and the faculty of reason in a broadly Platonic theory of knowledge: Perhaps no such unification is possible. In any case, the result in Descartes's writings is unacceptable as a philosophy of mind, and any innocent Cartesianism must revise unreconstructed Cartesianism significantly. One way in which this can be done is by deemphasising the elements of the theory of mind and body that are required to show that the soul does not die with the body, and to expand those that contribute to an account of the live human being.

An important passage for understanding the connection between the theory of mind and body on the one hand, and immortality on the other, is the following:

> Now the first and most important prerequisite for knowledge of the immortality of the soul is for us to form a concept of the soul which is as clear as possible and is also quite distinct from every concept of body; and that is just what has been done in [Meditation Two]. A further requirement is that we should know that everything that we clearly and distinctly understand is true in a way that corresponds exactly to our understanding . . . [A]ll the things that we clearly and distinctly perceive of as different substances (as we do in the case of mind and body) are in fact substances which are really distinct from one another; and this conclusion is drawn in the Sixth Meditation. This conclusion is confirmed . . . by the fact that we cannot understand a body except as being divisible, while by contrast we cannot understand a mind except as being indivisible. For we cannot conceive of half a mind, while we can always conceive of half a body, however small; and this leads us to recognize that the natures of mind and body are not only different, but in some way opposite. . . . The human body, insofar as it differs from other bodies, is simply made up of a certain configuration of limbs and other accidents of this sort; whereas the human mind is not made up of any accidents in this way, but is a pure substance. For even if all of the accidents of the mind change, so that it has different objects of the understanding and different desires and sensations, it does not on that account become a different mind; while the human body changes its identity merely as a result of a change in the shape of its parts. And from this it follows that while the body can very easily perish, the mind is immortal by its very nature. (CSM II 9–10; ATVII 13–14)

Descartes's idea seems to be that the individual mind is as enduring or eternal as matter in general, which is always conserved and in that sense always 'survives' in physical transactions. So the individual mind and matter in general contrast with the individual body, which is highly changeable and unstable in identity. Much of Descartes's detailed argument here is disputable: A change in the 'accidents' of the mind *can* raise questions about the identity of the relevant personality. It can count against a claim of psychological continuity and, to that extent, the identity through time of the relevant mind. Again, the divisibility of mind is partly provided for by Descartes's or anyone's anatomization of the mind into various mental faculties. In any case, the motivation for Descartes's substantial dualism seems to be largely theological: The more distinct mind (soul) and body are, the less the requirements for the survival of the one are involved with the survival of the other, and so the more it is a possibility that the soul does survive, whatever the body does. This is as close to an argument for the immortality of the soul as Descartes ever gets.

No innocent Cartesianism in the sense of this book can contain a theory of the mind significantly bent to the requirements of seventeenth-century Catholicism: To the extent that Descartes's insistence on the gulf between the concepts of the mind and the physical is theologically motivated, that insistence has to be dropped. The 'pure substance' that Descartes mentions in the passage just quoted is surely suspect. Descartes does better in the account of the survival and flourishing of human beings – that is, the survival of a human life or the union of a mind and body over a period of time. The theory of mind–body union is still a theory of distinct substances, and so it is still dualistic. But it is a dualism of connected and compatible and cooperating substances that reason in a self helps to perfect or improve. Having a reasonable life span and living well while one is alive depend for Descartes on a coordination and accommodation between an individual mind and body. Part of this consists of the living self's identifying itself with its body as well as with its mind. As Descartes's *Passions of the Soul* shows, there is no living well without the soul's attending to the conservation of the body and without the body's alerting the soul through sensation to sources of harm and benefit. In short, the mind and body, while distinct, are supposed to be able to operate in harmony, through therapies and rational precepts discovered by a Cartesian psychology and medicine. Even when the mind and body do not operate in harmony, they interact in regular ways. This is what makes each human being a unity of mind and body, and why, in ordinary life, the attribution of extension to the soul is excusable or even legitimate (CSM III 228; AT III 694), though in metaphysical strictness the soul has nothing to do with extension. The possibility of an individual body and mind working as a unity is as much part of God's creation as the pure substance of mind 'opposed' to the quasi-substance of the individual human body. Perhaps in Descartes's book the opposition between mind and body is more fundamental than the temporary harmony permitted by temporary union, but both are real.

What is Descartes's theory of mind–body union? He has a scientific hypothesis about where sensory input via animal motion to the brain from different sources is collected (the pineal gland), and he thinks it is by activity at the collecting point rather than elsewhere in the body that animal motion affects the mind. Beyond that, the theory of mind–body union is largely an explanation of how sensation, both external and internal, works. The theory indicates within what limits these sensations are sources of reliable knowledge of the external world and of the state of our bodies, and it tells us at the same time what good it does us to have these sensations – that is, how they aid survival. The internal sensations include feelings of hunger and thirst, pain, illness, pleasure, bodily movement, and the position at a time of our limbs. It is important to Descartes's theory that for human beings there is something it is like to be hungry, in pain, moving, sitting with one's legs crossed, and so on, and that we are acquainted with these phenomena immediately and from the inside. We do not normally find out we are hungry as a result of observation or investigation. When Descartes says, in both the *Meditations* and the *Discourse*, that we are not present in our bodies in exactly the way that a pilot is present in a ship (CSM II 56; AT VII 81; CSM I 141; AT VI 59), he has this point in mind. Similarly when he says that '*ambulo; ergo sum*' might do as well as '*cogito; ergo sum*' (CSM II 244; AT VII 352): Bodily movement of that kind is self-intimating. Descartes denies that the self-intimatingness of internal sensations is a reason for supposing that the relation of mind to body is thorough intermingling (as opposed to interaction of some kind through the pineal gland). Nevertheless, his physiological theories are supposed to help explain why the relation of a person to his or her own body is not the same as the relation of that person to a nearby body. Part of the explanation is that, typically, the objects of internal sensations are things going on *inside* the body, or on sensitive body surfaces – that is, in places connected to sensory receptors, while external bodies, especially moving or distant ones, can evade or stay out of range of the senses and may never be connected to the sensory receptors. Even nearby external bodies can fail to be noticed because the sensory receptors are not connected to them. But the connection is only part of the story. Just as important for Descartes is the fact that the sensations arising from question one can do no better than pinch oneself or raise one's arm having decided to do it. A theory that does not exclude physical realisation of conscious states is not necessarily a theory that *explains* the physical realisation of conscious states. Descartes's theory of the vital functions and of internal and external sensations does not presuppose a mind's having nothing to do with extension or matter; on the contrary. That does not mean, however, that it can do better than reply in silence to the question of how mind–body union or interaction is possible, or reduce conscious experience to something that it does not take experience to understand.

Descartes's silence in response to the question of the workings of union – his claim that there is in a sense no understanding that union – looks forward to two strands in the current philosophy of mind that are not commonly associated with Descartes but that may deserve to be included in an updated Cartesianism. One is the claim that we will never have the concepts to understand mind–body union: mysterianism. Another is that we do not *yet* have the concepts to understand mind–body union, though acquiring them or inventing them may not be impossible: mitigated mysterianism. Twenty-first-century mysterianism is sometimes rendered unstable by commitment to the idea that future concepts from physics or, more generally, the natural sciences, must fill the conceptual gap. A more stable mysterianism leaves open the question of the kind of concepts that are needed.

TOWARDS INNOCENT CARTESIANISM

If substantial dualism is subtracted from Descartes's theory of sensations and the vital functions, there is still a remainder. There is the not-so-innocent-looking thesis that internal and external sensations are, along with many other, or perhaps all, mental states, self-intimating, which helps to qualify them as Cartesian 'thoughts' – and there is the thesis that internal sensations are the best medium we have for grasping how mind and body can form a unity. This much is *fairly* innocent Cartesianism. It combines a kind of modesty in claims about the intelligibility through theory of mind–body union, with the idea that there is essentially something it is like to have sensations. In twentieth-century philosophy of mind we have the related position that there are limits to the understanding of mind–body identity, combined with the idea that

the best way of understanding some mental states may be by reference
to what it is like to be in them.

One philosophy of mind that incorporates most of this is Galen
Strawson's in *Mental Reality*. He inclines towards counting as mental
only conscious experiences or thoughts with a conscious aspect.[9] Dispositional beliefs and other dispositional propositional attitudes are
coherently excluded, he claims, because they do not intrinsically have
any content and, according to him, all mental states are intrinsically
'contentful'.[10] Again, he denies that in the classification or description
of mental states any reference to behaviour is essential.[11] On the other
hand, he finds it hard to deny that the mental is to be explained by
the nonmental, specifically the physical. Only 'hard to deny' because
he does not think he can prove it: Various versions of idealism that
he cannot exclude stand in the way of asserting that the explanation
of the mental is physical or material.[12] Though Strawson's position
is materialist, it is also supposed to be modest. He does not think, as
perhaps some physicists do, that physics is the theory of everything.
Strawson doubts that physics as we currently understand it is capable
of encompassing the mental; on the contrary, he anticipates that significant amounts of conceptual revision of current physics will need to
pave the way for any physical explanation of the mental that deserves
the name.[13]

Because he supposes that the sphere of the mental coincides
with the sphere of the experiential or the conscious, Strawson's position is much more robustly Cartesian than others. But it is also
significantly non-Cartesian: for according to Strawson, 'experiential
phenomena ... are entirely physical phenomena'.[14] It is in virtue of
this last materialistic aspect of his position that Strawson calls it 'naturalistic Cartesianism'. Enlarging on his materialism, Strawson writes:

My faith, like that of many other materialists, consists in a bundle of connected
and unverifiable beliefs. I believe that experience is not all there is to reality.
I believe that there is a physical world that involves the existence of space and

[9] *Mental Reality*, pp. 162ff.
[10] Ibid., pp. 166ff.
[11] Ibid., ch. 8.
[12] Ibid., ch. 5.
[13] *Mental Reality*, p. 104.
[14] Ibid., p. 318.

space-occupying entities that have non-experiential properties. I believe that the theory of evolution is true, that once there was no experience like ours on this planet, whether pansychism is true or false, and that there came to be experience like ours as a result of processes that at no point involved anything not wholly physical or material in nature. . . . Experience is as much a physical phenomenon as electric charge.[15]

This faith sits uneasily with the claim that physics stands in need of conceptual revision. If the resources of physics are inadequate to encompass the mental, so must the concept of the physical be. How, then, can that concept turn out to be adequate on the strength of anything evolutionary theory says? The concept of the physical associated with evolutionary theory surely cannot have any more authority than the concepts of physics that require revision. So if evolutionary theory confines the processes that created mind to those that are purely physical or material, and we are not sure what the physical is or includes, we do not know what the process of evolution includes or excludes either. In any case, even if the mechanisms that produced biological life, including consciousness, are, at some level, the *same* as those that operate in the evolution of the physical universe, it does not follow that those mechanisms are physical just because physical evolution preceded biological evolution. Perhaps some transphysical and transmental concept is required to capture both mechanisms. This conjecture stakes out a territory for something sometimes called "neutral monism" in addition to dualist, physicalist, and idealist positions.

Strawson raises the question whether neutral monism is the right response to the failure up to now of physicalism to encompass the mental, and his answer appears to be 'No', on the ground that preferring neutral monism to the other available positions implies that physical categories have no very great explanatory power and perhaps none at all. Strawson associates neutral monism with the view that 'we have definitely not managed to attain any sort of knowledge of the nature of reality in our use of our actual categories of the mental and the physical'.[16] But this does not seem to be implied by neutral monism. The fact that there may be some as yet undreamt up concept or conceptual domain capable of unifying the mental and the physical

---

[15] Ibid., p. 105.
[16] Ibid., p. 98.

does not mean that nothing is explained by physical concepts. It means only that physical concepts are not ultimate. Such a view seems to be on the cards as soon as one says that the concepts of physics may require radical revision, without imposing limits on the revision.

As Spinoza saw, Descartes's own position leaves room for something like neutral monism, for it contains a concept of substance that is transmental and transphysical, but one that Descartes does not elaborate to any great degree, and that Spinoza tries to elaborate for him. Not only does Descartes's concept of substance invite appropriation by the neutral monist: so does the phenomenon of the union between mind and body, which Descartes says we have access to only through experience. Perhaps we have access to it only through experience because the necessary concepts have yet to be provided by metaphysics, and the metaphysics that Descartes has elaborated is not a complete metaphysics. This reading of Descartes puts Strawson's agnostic materialism in close proximity to original Cartesianism, for, like Descartes, Strawson thinks that concepts of physics give us some knowledge of the natures of things, but not a knowledge of all of the natures of things. On the other hand, Descartes's own Cartesianism is by no means a naturalistic Cartesianism, because some of the natures of things left out of physics are the natures of things outside nature. As for Strawson, he says that the concept of the natural is no more determinate or well understood than the concept of the physical, and, that being so, he cannot consistently think that the subject matter of naturalism or, therefore, of a naturalistic Cartesianism can be determinate either. It is unclear what work 'naturalistic' does, then, except that of begging the question whether concepts sufficient to encompass the mental and the physical will be physical.

This is more than a dispute about words. A lot of the controversy between the antireductionists and the eliminativists in the philosophy of mind assumes that physics is in perfectly good order, and naturalism usually means regarding as real only what can exist consistently with whatever current physics is committed to. To leave room for something that might succeed physics without discrediting physics, therefore, seems to me to push at the limits of naturalism. The things room is left for need not be in the least spooky. After all, mathematical objects can be well understood – through the postulates, definitions, axioms, and theorems of geometry and number theory – even if they are not the subject of a physical theory. This may have been Descartes's thought, too. When he says that metaphysics is the science of immaterial things he does not mean finite minds and the divine mind only: He recognises the existence of, for example, the natures of triangles, which are 'immutable and eternal, and not invented by me or dependent on my mind' (CSM II 45; AT VII 64). Perhaps transphysical concepts are required quite independently of the irreducibility of the mind: because *mathematical* and physical objects are independently real. If so, this is another element of an innocent Cartesianism, and to the extent a naturalised Cartesianism does not accommodate it, it seems to me not to be open minded enough.

NATURALISM AND 'EXISTENTIAL NATURALISM'

Naturalism is what makes the mind–body problem *seem* soluble to the reductionists; naturalism is also what makes its apparent insolubility disturbing to antireductionists. According to those who think that consciousness can't be explained, the inexplicability is paradoxical: It *ought* to be possible to explain it, and explain it naturalistically, for, after all, consciousness is part of biological evolution. According to those on the other side of the debate, 'ought' implies 'can'. If consciousness is natural, then it *is* possible to explain it naturalistically; it is just difficult to do so.

I believe that the deference to naturalism is overdone even by those who think that consciousness is inexplicable. Colin McGinn has tried to define and defend a kind of naturalism consistent with the belief that the way that consciousness depends on matter cannot be explained.[17] What he calls 'existential naturalism' is the thesis that

nothing that happens in nature is inherently anomalous, God-driven, an abrogation of basic laws – whether or not we can come to comprehend the processes at work.[18]

In particular, *something* in nature makes consciousness arise from the brain, but this something, according to McGinn, is permanently inaccessible to us. Consciousness is different in this respect from a vast

[17] My discussion is based on Chapter 3 of *The Problem of Consciousness*, pp. 44–88.
[18] Ibid., p. 87.

array of natural kinds of physical object – whose superficial properties do have an accessible basis in different types of microstructure. The success that physics has had in identifying these microstructures has encouraged a belief in what McGinn contrasts with existential natural- ism, namely 'effective naturalism'. Effective naturalism is

the thesis that we should be able to provide or construct naturalistic accounts of every phenomenon in nature: we should be able actually to specify naturalistic necessary and sufficient conditions for the phenomenon in question.[19]

A belief in global effective naturalism is a kind of intellectual hubris, McGinn says, and I agree. But the apparently more modest existential naturalism is presumptuous in its own way. For while it supposes (mod- estly enough) that we will never know what cements consciousness to matter, it seems to insist that the unintelligible cement is material or physical – what else could come under law? No attempt is made to widen the application of 'natural' beyond the physical. But if the for- ever missing concepts for the hidden nature of consciousness can be pronounced in advance to be physical, how radically unintelligible are they? After all, it cannot be said that we don't know the first thing about the physical. Either McGinn can be a mysterian with respect to consciousness, or a naturalist, but not both.

Twentieth-century mysterianism is anticipated up to a point in Descartes, for it seems to follow from Descartes's claims about the limits of the human understanding of the union between mind and body that the basis for the union is not available to the human intellect. The union is partially available to experience, but not in the form of a sense-based conception awaiting correction by something better. For Descartes, the internal senses put the mind in touch with a fact – that the mind is connected to the body – in a way that the external senses fail to when they suggest that colour or smell inheres in an external body. The secondary qualities do not really inhere in the bodies, and the explanation of colour experience or odour will refer only to the way that bodies disturb parts of the eye or nose and their connections to the brain. The mind, by contrast, really does inhere – somehow – in the body as long as a human being is alive, and so the experience of embodiment is not in need of correction or of explaining away,

[19] Ibid.

except inasmuch as it suggests a thorough intermingling of the mind and body. There is no thorough intermingling, only the functioning of the pineal gland. In other words, the inherence of the mind in the body is not a permeation. But a reference to the connection between the mind and the body is essential to the explanation of internal sensation.

On the other hand, the inherence of the mind in a body in any form – even in the sense of a mental receptor constituted by the pineal gland – is metaphysically odd on Descartes's assumptions. According to Descartes, embodiment is not essential to being a mind. On the contrary, the most perfect mind – God's – has nothing to do with a body. Even the much less capable human mind does not *have* to have anything to do with a body, and, according to Descartes, its having something to do with the body renders it less capable than it might be, renders it less than perfect as the limited sort of mind it is. In this respect, the embodiment of the human mind, while real, is unnecessary *and* unfortunate. It needs explaining twice over. Given that it is not in the nature of the mind to be embodied, and that embodiment handicaps the mind, why is the human mind embodied at all? Second, *how* is it embodied? Both questions express mysteries, and the second is a version of twenty-first-century mysterianism in the philosophy of mind.

Descartes's mysterianism is conspicuously less naturalistic than the mysterianism of today. For him, the most perfect mind, the thing that a mind ought most to be, is eternal, uncaused, and disembodied – in short, non-natural. It is also the source of nature, and therefore strongly supernatural. Twenty-first-century mysterians do not usually work with the notion of a perfect mind, still less with the idea that the perfect – that is, the divine – mind sets the pattern for mentality in general. On the other hand, they do work with a conception of the mind that is much broader than the conception of the human mind. Their concept of the mind and, in particular, of consciousness, has to extend to nonhumans on Earth, and to extraterrestrials, whose biology may have little in common with ours. Even for extraterrestrials, however, mysterians assume that matter predates the mind, including consciousness, and that it has arisen somehow with or from matter in the relevant part of the universe. Descartes, I think defensibly, separates the nature of the mind from its evolutionary history, and from its role in mediating between bodily sensory stimulus and behaviour. It is important to his account, and true independently, that a mind does not cease to be a mind if it lacks physical sensation. It is important to his account, and not obviously false, that a mind is no less a mind if it has only the capacity to think abstractly and to will general policies of action, like the mind of the god of the philosophers.

This concept of mind probably does not fit mortal creatures on this or other planets, who have to devise means to ends in specific situations or else perish, but it does *overlap* with concepts that fit mortal creatures – that is, concepts of mind that include capacities for abstract as well as situational thinking and willing. A theory of the abstract-minded does not necessarily have to posit a seat for the abstract mind in the thick of a stimulus-and-response mechanism. And Descartes's theory does not. It is true that this poses problems for Descartes, even in the case of God. For if an abstract infinite mind is not to be restricted to contemplation, if it is also to play the role of the biblical god, it has got to have a place in, or be identical with, the causal nexus. But there is no necessary connection between the abstract mind and the biblical, intervening god, just as there is no necessary connection between the abstract mind and the active, place-, and time-bound mortal creature. Descartes's theory of the mind does identify an abstract-minded god with the biblical god. But it seems intelligible as a mind anyway, without that identification. We do seem to be able to grasp the idea of an all-comprehending, non-intervening abstract intelligence. We do seem to be able to conceive of a finite non-intervening abstract mind as well. Differently, we can conceive of a mind imprisoned in a paralysed or unresponsive body. This is not the mind of a fully fledged agent, or even of an agent with properties that suit it to survive and reproduce its kind. It is not a mind, then, that has a place in any plausible evolutionary story. Neither has a purely contemplative mind a place in such a story. Both sorts of mind exceed the limits of naturalism. But they are for all that minds.

Because our concept of the mind is non-naturalistic in part, the non-naturalism of Descartes's account makes it able to recover parts of our concept of mind that other accounts do not reach. Descartes's account also sits better with mysterianism, for it need not, perhaps incoherently, prejudge the materials of the account of the mind–body relation that we can never arrive at. It can be neutral about the materials.

In particular, it need not assume that the mind–body relation will be reconstructed with as yet undeveloped physical concepts. The insufficiency of naturalism for solving the mind–body problem has counterparts in the inadequacy of naturalistic approaches to other philosophical problems. For example, there is a longstanding problem in philosophy of mathematics over whether mathematical realism can be naturalised. On the one hand, it does not do to say that mathematical entities exist only to the extent that they are indispensable for physics, or that mathematical statements are meaningful or true only to the extent that physics finds a use for them. On the other hand, it seems unsatisfactory to say that the objects and theorems of mathematics are objective and independent of the mind in some hard-to-specify way that the truths of physics are not, and that they are accessible to a hard-to-describe mathematical intuition quite different from ordinary perception.[20] But the latter claims, despite their mystery, are at least consistent with some of the phenomenology and practice of mathematics, including elementary mathematics. They seem to accommodate the immediate obviousness of elementary mathematics in the way the indispensability account does not; they also accommodate the autonomy of mathematical methods of defending mathematical claims, notably formal proof. Physics and its methods of verification seem irrelevant to whether we accept elementary mathematics, which has its own, independent claims to objectivity, truth, and acceptance. Indeed, elementary mathematics was justifiably accepted before there was a mathematical physics; and physics and its methods also seem irrelevant to the acceptability among specialists of esoteric mathematical claims.[21] The autonomy of the mathematical may not be *illuminated* by Godelian or Platonist realism; but at least it is not denied. A kind of agnosticism or mysterianism may be in order until, if ever, something better than the Godelian or Platonic approach can be found. Here, too, naturalism cannot simply be *assumed* to be adequate.

An approach to the mind–body relation that avoids a narrow naturalism as well as some of the difficulties of McGinn's formulation

---

[20] This position is associated in the twentieth century with Godel. The indispensability-to-physics version of mathematical realism is due to Quine and Putnam. I rely heavily on the account given in Penelope Maddy's *Naturalism in Mathematics* (Oxford: Oxford University Press, 1997), chs. 1–6.

[21] Maddy, p. 106.

but leaves room for mysterianism is Thomas Nagel's in *The View from Nowhere*.[22] This is a departure from his proposal of objective phenomenology in 'What is it like to be a Bat?'[23] In *The View from Nowhere*, Nagel is looking not for concepts that will apply to both sides of psychophysical identity statements but rather for a concept that the *self* can come under, such that that concept is of something whose objective persistence is believed aposteriori to be a necessary condition of the continuity of the self. The 'objective completion' of the concept of the self is a concept for something capable of having a point of view, thus guarding against one sort of reduction, but it is also general, and many things might be believed to satisfy it. Nagel compares objective completion of the concept of the self to the objective completion of the concept of gold. '[B]efore the development of chemistry, "gold" already referred to a type of metal, and this determined which kind of further discoveries about its material composition would reveal the true nature of gold'.[24] The concept that does for the self what the concept of a metal did for gold is the concept of the whole, full-functioning brain.[25] This form of approach still leaves residues of mystery, mainly to do with how the unity of the mind can be reconciled with the idea that human beings are combinations of arbitrary selections of matter, but the added difficulties of surface and depth of consciousness made so much of by McGinn are not among them. Furthermore, Nagel's proposal is open-minded in a way I earlier complained Galen Strawson's wasn't. It makes room for something in the area of neutral monism. Nagel writes that 'if both mental and physical aspects of a process are manifestations of something more fundamental, the mental need not entail the physical nor vice versa even if both are entailed by this something else.'[26] This is the possibility left open by Spinoza's take

---

[22] (Oxford: Clarendon Press, 1986), pp. 37ff.

[23] According to Nagel, mind–brain identity need not remain forever unintelligible for us, but we would need new concepts for any proposed reductive identification to make sense, that, at a first approximation, would be concepts for what mental states are objectively *like*. So he does not anticipate a direct application of physical concepts to experiences like pain – as in current versions of physicalism – but at best an application of physical concepts to whatever the concepts of an "objective phenomenology" – a theory of what experiences are objectively like – apply to (loc. cit., p. 178).

[24] Ibid., p. 39.

[25] Ibid., p. 40

[26] Ibid., p. 48.

on Cartesianism, and it is probably something that any satisfactory mysterian proposal must make room for.

Nagel's proposal has been further refined since the appearance of *The View from Nowhere*. In 'Conceiving the Impossible and the Mind-Body Problem',[27] he applies the approach of objective completability to the concept of mind itself and says that the completed concept of the mental has to pick out something that will simultaneously satisfy functionalism, physicalism, and the irreducibility of the first-person point of view. More than that, it will have to entail as impossible what, in the poverty of the current concept of mind, we seem to be able to conceive: zombies. On the other hand, it will permit as necessary what first-person intuitions seem to suggest is merely contingent: the relation of C-fibre firing and pain. The successor concept to the concept of mind will thus permit a uniform account of a whole range of material that has been spawned by the mind–body problem. Nagel likens the role of the new concept to that of field in physics. Just as the concept of the field was able to unify mechanical and electrico-magnetic phenomena, the completed concept of the mental would unite the mental and physical – a far more fundamental sort of unification. It would be the key to a sort of empirical neutral monism.

This version of neutral monism dispenses with some central Cartesian notions while retaining others. It insists on the ineliminability of the first-person point of view; but it does not insist on its incorrigibility or on the authority of modal claims inspired by it. Thus, it allows that the apparent conceivability of pain without C-fibre firing may be merely apparent. It also seems to dispense with the unreconstructed Cartesian idea that the mind is better known than the body. For if it is a single as yet undeveloped concept that is going to throw light on the mind–body problem, and if our current concept of the mind is incomplete, and if we have no idea as yet how to complete it, then in that sense we do not fully know the mind. And if part of what the developed concept of the mind is supposed to do is to take into account and square with what we know of the correlations between mental functioning and brain anatomy, then the understanding of the mind will, once again contrary to Descartes, call upon far more than the concept of thought.

---

[27] *Philosophy* 73 (1998), pp. 337–52.

It is not clear whether this or any other form of neutral monism will be able to deal with another sort of dualism – namely that between the abstract and the concrete. Were a neutral monism like Nagel's to be worked out, it would show what kind of single reality made room for both the mental and the physical. But would it show what kind of single reality could accommodate, in addition to the mental and the physical, the abstract in general, the mathematical in particular? It is hard to say in advance. But the Cartesian picture of the two worlds, which neutral monism is supposed to eliminate, traditionally co-exists with the trialism of the mathematical (or abstract), the mental and the physical. Certainly the Fregean third world of 'The Thought' seems to be anticipated in Meditation 5. Descartes unifies these worlds unsatisfactorily by making the abstract (e.g., geometrical simple natures) an artifact of God alongside minds and bodies. Naturalistic realists try to unify the three realms by saying that anything exists that needs to be quantified over in the most explanatory overall theory of nature. But this probably underrepresents the reasons we have for committing ourselves to mathematical entities. Perhaps we need to commit ourselves to them to account for the truth of simple arithmetic and the phenomenology of mathematical thought and discovery. If this is right, there must still be a role for a metaphysical monism beyond an empirical neutral monism. This might fit into a first philosophy, even if not quite a first philosophy as Descartes conceived it.

REACTIONS TO IRREDUCIBILITY CLAIMS

Unlike outright mysterianism, Nagel's account assumes only that the mind–body problem is *currently* intractable. Even this can seem dogmatic to people who are pursuing empirical research in the brain sciences, or to those in philosophy who support this research and are trying to work out a philosophy of mind that keeps up with it. These scientists and philosophers do not see why the postulation of a mechanism underlying sensory experience cannot contribute to an account of the nature of consciousness. And some of them respond to the claim that a purely physical account of consciousness must leave something out by asking why a purely physical account of biological life seems *not* to leave anything out. Mysterianism, or, more generally, opposition to reductionist accounts of consciousness, seems to some to repeat the excesses of vitalism.[28] The alleged parallel is worth discussing, as it brings out many of the issues concerning explanatory adequacy and explanatory gaps that seem to divide the antireductionist from the reductionists. After distinguishing vitalism from mysterianism, I shall consider briefly a final objection to latter-day Cartesian positions from those who believe in subpersonal accounts of consciousness.

Vitalism is the view that some special, irreducible life force is needed to organise mere inert matter into a living organism and to endow it with some of the characteristic biological functions.[29] This view has effectively been superseded by modern genetics. The unit of heredity – the gene – encodes the instructions for cells and organisms to replicate and is made up of DNA, chains of four types of nucleotides. Genes make proteins that contribute to the formation of the specialised cells – nerve, muscle, and skin cells, for example – that underlie many of the pretheoretically recognised organs and capacities and functions of the whole organism. No account of how the genes do their work needs to invoke a vital force, and the physical character of cells and their constituents is not in doubt. Why is this not a model for how a future brain science could excise references to conscious experience?

Some answers distinguish life from consciousness; others distinguish the explanatory gaps that vitalists believed would be permanent from the explanatory gaps involved in explaining how consciousness could arise from the brain. Although I believe that some of these answers are on the right lines, some are not. Here is McGinn on the difference between life and consciousness:

Reproduction involves causal processes that are continuously biological: at no stage does the organic lapse into the inorganic, only to regain life further down the line. If there were such a break, then reproduction would have to achieve

---

[28] See for example Dennett, 'Facing Backwards on the Problem of Consciousness' in Shear, ed., *Explaining Consciousness*, op. cit., pp. 33–6.

[29] In fairness to the consciousness/brain reductionists, it must be conceded that some of their opponents do *seem* to reproduce the rhetoric of 'mere inert matter'. McGinn writes, 'Brains seem very similar to other parts of animal bodies, being basically a big collection of cells organized according to biochemical principles. Yet there is a yawning chasm between the natures of those entities, because brains produce consciousness and those other meaty organs do not, not even a little bit' (*The Mysterious Flame*, op. cit., p. 9). Part of the rhetorical force of this passage is that the *look* of all of these organs makes the production of consciousness unlikely. A page earlier, McGinn is saying 'how surprising it is that the squishy grey matter in our heads – our brain meat – can be the basis and cause of such a rich mental life'.

the equivalent of the beginning of evolution each time a new organism was produced....

But in the case of consciousness that is exactly what we do get. When one centre of consciousness produces another, there is a period when the process of consciousness is interrupted: indeed, the capacity for consciousness is not present during this period ... So when consciousness finally dawns in a developing organism it does not stem from an immediately prior consciousness; it stems from oblivion.[30]

Matter and life both stand in opposition to consciousness in this respect, according to McGinn; for just as we do not have to posit a lot of beginnings of evolution to explain the birth of a succession of new organisms, 'we do not have to posit lots of Little Big Bangs to account for freshly minted physical objects'. But nothing stands to consciousness as the Big Bang stands to matter.

The discontinuity McGinn makes so much of – 'when one centre of consciousness produces another' – is no more to be described as creation from oblivion or as involving radical discontinuity than the process that leads from the copulation of a brain-bearing couple to the formation of the brain in their offspring. It is true that for a long time after conception there is no brain, but that does not mean that when the brain does arise, or when it starts functioning, either of those things arises from oblivion. By the same token, it is unnecessary to speak of consciousness arising from oblivion: It comes into existence with brain functioning. Or to put it in a different way, one centre of consciousness can produce another only in the way one biological organism with sentience produces another that develops to the right point. The discontinuity is no more striking than organisms' not producing their kind in immediately very developed form. Contrary to McGinn, there is probably a pretty *good* analogy between the rise of life and the rise of consciousness in an individual.

But this doesn't mean that consciousness is open to a naturalistic explanation without remainder, in the way that life is. Chalmers is better than McGinn on the difference between vitalism and the belief that consciousness is not open to physical reduction:

What drove vitalist skepticism was doubt about whether physical mechanisms could perform the many remarkable functions associated with life, such as

---

[30] *The Problem of Consciousness*, op. cit., p. 46.

complex adaptive behavior and reproduction. The conceptual claim that explanation of functions is what is needed was implicitly accepted, but lacking detailed knowledge of biochemical mechanisms, vitalists doubted whether any physical process could do the job, and put forward the hypothesis of the vital spirit as an alternative explanation. . . .

With experience, on the other hand, the physical explanation of the functions is not in question. The key is instead the *conceptual* point that the explanation of functions does not suffice for the explanation of experience. . . . In a similar way, experience is disanalogous to the *elan vital.* . . . Experience is not an explanatory posit but an explanadum in its own right, and so is not a candidate for [the same sort of elimination as vital spirit].[31]

Experience is not some sort of theoretical entity. We don't make references to it only in order to explain things. On the contrary, first-person references to it are hardly ever explanatory. There also appears to be something irreducibly personal as opposed to subpersonal about experiences. That is why the reduction of experience to subpersonal processes on the model of the reduction of elan vital to cellular processes seems so forlorn.

This last point, however, also tells against Chalmers's own, allegedly *non*-reductive explanation of experience: one that posits, as a basic principle, a phenomenal and a physical aspect to states of information. If the existence of a phenomenal aspect of information means an aspect for a person, this will involve a 'high-level notion' of awareness that Chalmers thinks must be got rid of in the basic principles of a theory of experience.[32] But how are phenomenal aspects to be understood, except through 'high-level' – that is, unreduced – notions? When Chalmers insists, correctly, that the explanation of functions does not explain experience as it explains life, and that this is a conceptual point, part of what makes for the explanatory shortfall is that vital functions, and therefore vital force, can be reduced to subpersonal processes, while the concept of experience apparently cannot. This apparent impossibility is not a simple failure of imagination, as some eliminativists claim.[33] On the other hand, there is a certain misleadingness

---

[31] 'Facing up to the Problem of Consciousness' in J. Shear, ed., *Explaining Consciousness: The Hard Problem* (Cambridge, Mass.: MIT Press, 1997), pp. 18–19.

[32] Ibid., p. 26.

[33] See Patricia Churchland, 'The Hornswoggle Problem' in Shear, ed., *Explaining Consciousness*, p. 42.

in putting the problem of consciousness as one of inexplicability, as if everything to do with consciousness had to be some sort of mystery or as if consciousness were scientifically quite inscrutable. Even the arch-mysterian McGinn does not deny that 'there is plenty of interesting and important work to be done in the neurophysiology of mind', by which he means, *inter alia*, work on determining 'just which neural properties determine whether the subject is in a conscious state'.[34] This work is supposed to be both possible and worthwhile without its helping with the question of how what-it's-likeness can spring at all from the brain or more generally from an arbitrary combination of material particles. A certain scientific programme is pursuable even if it does not answer every question about the relation of mind and body, and even if the *fundamental* question is not addressed. Vast amounts of routine physics also lie outside cosmology.

It is Chalmers who sometimes describes the pursuable scientific programme or programmes as fraudulent because they do not address, let alone solve, the question of why there is or how there can be experience at all.[35] Chalmers distinguishes the pursuable scientific questions from the intractable questions by labelling the former 'easy' and the latter 'hard'. These obviously unfortunate labels have prompted scepticism about the reality of the distinction to which they are applied. Not only are the easy problems arguably far less than easy; some of the supposedly easy – that is, scientifically tractable – questions do seem to have a bearing on the hard question, even if they do not fully answer it. For example, the question of how a 'system' is able to access its own inner states and how it is able to attend to things are among Chalmers's easy questions. It is hard to deny that an ability to attend is normally part of what it is to be conscious. A theory that enables us to move from talk of undifferentiated consciousness to different kinds of attention and their physical basis is not irrelevant to the question of how consciousness is possible, for it makes the explanandum more specific. It can indeed do more. A theory that correlates smell, taste, and colour experience with the patterns of stimulation of specific receptor cells on the relevant sense organs can be extremely informative – explanatory in a clear sense and yet still not answer every important question in the

[34] *The Mysterious Flame*, op. cit., p. 70.
[35] 'Facing up to the Problem of Consciousness', pp. 9–18.

field, including how there can be introspective experience at all, or, differently, why more of what we experience should not be 'processed' subliminally. On the other hand, those questions it does answer are not necessarily 'easy'.

One way of summarising Chalmers's thesis and what is wrong with it is by saying that for him experience resists theoretical elimination in the form of an identification of a mechanism – as if explanation consisted *only* of theoretical elimination through the identification of a mechanism. This is certainly the view of eliminative materialists, but, like Chalmers's, their view does not easily accommodate the idea that explanation in the area we are considering can be real while being incomplete.[36] Innocent Cartesianism does accommodate this idea, while providing reasons for thinking that explanation by the identification of a mechanism *must* be incomplete. It must be incomplete, because it cannot encompass all of the data and be wholly subpersonal – experience is something for a *whole subject* – and because many states of the subpersonal mechanism do not appear to have phenomenal qualities at all. The fully functioning *whole* brain *is* a possible subject of experience. It is identifiable in principle with a pretheoretical self in a way the cones on the retina or the retina itself cannot begin to be. The innocent Cartesianism of Nagel goes this far with materialism, while denying that we yet have the concepts that make the identity intelligible. But the fully functioning whole brain is not one of the relata of the identities that identity theorists usually have in mind.

---

[36] I do not include David Chalmers among the innocent Cartesians. Although he sometimes associates his views with those of writers like Nagel, McGinn, and Strawson, his understanding of what the hard problem of consciousness is, is different from theirs. Chalmers wonders why there should be auditory experience or colour experience rather than an exclusively subpersonal subliminal sensitivity to air vibration and reflected light (see 'Facing up to the Problem of Consciousness', pp. 10–11). This is a good question, but not the makings of the mind–body problem, which is closer to the question of how auditory and colour experience can arise from the brain. Occasionally, as in the opening lines of his book *The Conscious Mind: In Search of a Fundamental Theory* (Oxford: Oxford University Press, 1996), Chalmers confuses the mind–body problem–hard problem with his own. Chalmers's theoretical response to his own hard problem of consciousness is what he calls 'naturalistic dualism'. This sounds like a Cartesian position, and to the extent it is dualistic it is, but it implies that phenomenal quality is physically *basic* and that physical states are information states, both of which seem far too contentious to qualify for what I am calling innocent Cartesianism.

I come now to the final objection. The whole-brain/self-identity mooted by Nagel is hardly Descartes's substantial dualism all over again, but is it innocent enough? Many think it cannot possibly be. According to Dennett, resistance to subpersonal theories of consciousness is the stubborn residue of Cartesianism even in those philosophers of mind willing to give computation and the brain their due:

> The chief source of the myth of the Cartesian Theatre, after all, is the lazy extrapolation of the intentional stance *all the way in.* Treating a complex, moving entity as a single-minded agent is a magnificent way of seeing pattern in all activity; the tactic comes naturally to us, and is probably even genetically favoured as a way of perceiving and thinking. But when we aspire to a science of the mind, we must learn to restrain and redirect those habits of thought, breaking the single-minded agent into mini agents and microagents (with no single Boss).[37]

According to Dennett, there are many different sources in the brain of discriminations that make a difference to subsequent behaviour, and therefore many different sources of conscious events. Only some of the after-effects of discriminations (of movement or colour, for example) will leave traces in memory or be registered in verbal behaviour, but these are not the only things that deserve to be called conscious events. The temptation to be restrictive in this way about what to call conscious events is partly encouraged by the idea (itself derived from Descartes) that there is some special junction in the brain where all information paths meet and pass into the mind – the pineal gland or some other favoured section of the brain. In fact there is no central point or control room in the brain, and the work of registering sensory stimulation and motor response is divided into a number of simultaneous operations areas.

What looks like a picture in Dennett of a plurality of outposts of consciousness is rather confusingly labelled a 'multiple drafts' model of consciousness,[38] as if what were at issue was whether information affecting behaviour were ever revised, rather than whether it had to form a single point of view. 'Multiple drafters' model or 'Multiple editors' model would be more apt, at least where the Cartesian position it is supposed to supersede is that there is always some unitary subject

---

[37] *Consciousness Explained* (London: Penguin, 1993), p. 458.
[38] *Consciousness Explained,* ch. 5.

for whom the information from the various parts of the brain has to be put together or some unitary subject who does the putting together. Dennett argues that even where an interpretation of experimental data appears to call for a Boss-beyond-the parts-of-the-brain to intervene to fill gaps or make inferences, no such figure is in fact needed to explain experimental data. Nor could one operate in the tiny spans of time it would appear to have to intervene. For example, a Boss appears to be needed to explain the *phi* effect involving two coloured spots. The *phi* effect is the illusion of a single dot moving from left to right when all the eyes see are two separate, stationary dots in quick succession. Two dots have to be seen for the illusion of a single moving dot to be created. When the two dots are different colours, the illusion is of a single dot moving from left to right and changing colour in mid-career. This seems to create a puzzle: How can the change to the colour of the second dot register before the second dot and the second dot's colour have been seen? One possibility: The brain registers the succession of dots, produces the illusion of the moving dot, and registers the difference in colour in a retrospective illusion of a change of a colour. Either that, or the brain registers the two different coloured spots separately *as* stationary, wipes out that memory, and substitutes for it the illusion of the moving colour-changing spot. Both hypotheses fit the data; neither calls for a further subject for whom the brain constructs the 'path' of the 'moving' dot in the monochrome *phi* experiment or the 'path' plus passage through the spectrum from the colour of the first dot to the colour of the second.[39] The further subject is as redundant as the idea that everything in consciousness is played out in the Cartesian theatre.

Because sometimes for Dennett the brain seems to play the role of the whole subject, even if there is no control room in the brain, it is not always clear how far the 'multiple' drafts story must be incompatible with the objective completion of the self as brain in Nagel. It is true that many things the brain or brain regions do are not things with phenomenal qualities. To that extent the substitution of the brain for the self seems to cut down on what-it's-likeness. But it was never Nagel's thesis or a thesis of innocent Cartesianism that everything which happens in the *mind*, let alone the brain, is self-intimating; the thesis is

[39] Ibid., p. 128.

5

Reason, Emotion, and Action

A Cartesian theory of the mind emphasises more than consciousness and the first person. It emphasises reason. In Descartes's own writings, reason is said to correct the deliverances of the senses and is supposed to be the main influence on belief. But it is also supposed to counterbalance the more body-based passions and to take precedence as an influence on action. Descartes is sometimes accused of overemphasising reason and exaggerating the antagonism between reason and other nonrational sources of action. Perhaps a neo-Cartesian theory of the mind is open to a similar accusation, because any Cartesian theory is inevitably rationalist. Might an excessive rationalism be expressed by the idea that reason is a self-sufficient sort of motivation, a proposer of means *and* ends, not the slave of the passions in the least? I consider this possibility later on in the chapter. I will argue that some form of belief in practical reason is both authentically Cartesian and innocent. I begin, however, with an error that is supposed to arise when Cartesian rationalism is taken together with dualism. What has been called 'Descartes's error'[1] is the supposition that embodiment is unnecessary for reasoning, feeling, or other aspects of mental life. Combining this error with the idea (also visible to some readers of Descartes) that emotion and rationality are more often in conflict than in harmony, one allegedly puts entirely out of reach a correct understanding and

[1] See Antonio R. Damasio, *Descartes's Error: Emotion, Reason and the Human Brain* (London: Picador, 1995).

successful treatment of brain disorders and injuries that produce an impaired rationality by altering emotional capacities. In this way, and in others that are more far-reaching, Cartesian ideas are supposed to be disabling for medicine.

DAMASIO'S ERROR

'Descartes's error' is a supposed mistake characterised by the neurologist Antonio Damasio. Damasio has a cognitive theory of emotions, a number of hypotheses about the systems of the brain responsible for emotional functioning, and is interested in the general relations between emotion and reason. Far from supposing that reason and emotion work against one another, and that reasoning works best in the absence of emotion, Damasio claims that the loss of emotional capacity can produce defective practical decision making.[2]

Two case studies dominate the book-length discussion that leads up to his identifying Descartes's error. One case goes back to the nineteenth century and concerns the well-documented effects of a serious brain injury arising from an accident in which an iron bar used for tamping explosives penetrated someone's skull at high speed. The victim of the accident, Phineas P. Gage, survived, but he suffered serious and disfiguring head injuries and underwent a radical personality change. The second case concerns a patient of Damasio's who had surgery for a brain tumour. His personality also changed. Both patients appeared to retain reasonably strong powers of memory, speech, attention, and reasoning. In Damasio's own patient 'Elliot', these powers were in fact formidable – far better than normal – as measured by a battery of recognised psychological tests. But neither Elliot nor Gage was able to take up the life he led before his brain damage. On the contrary, they lost their ability to give appropriate weight in their decisions to their immediate projects, or their longer-term futures; and their success in maintaining their relationships with those around them was severely reduced. Before the brain damage, each was highly productive, with a successful work and family life. After the brain damage, each patient went into dramatically steep decline.

---

[2] Ibid., p. 45; p. 51.

The character of the decline in Gage is described like this. (The passages in single quotation marks are from the account of John Harlow, who was Gage's doctor):

As Harlow recounts, the 'equilibrium or balance, so to speak, between his intellectual faculty and animal propensities' had been destroyed. The changes became apparent as soon as the acute phase of brain injury subsided. He was now 'fitful, irreverent, indulging at times in the grossest profanity which was not previously his custom, manifesting but little deference for his fellows, impatient of restraint or advice when it conflicts with his desires, at times pertinaciously obstinate, yet capricious and vacillating, devising many plans of future operation, which are no sooner arranged than they are abandoned . . . A child in intellectual capacity and manifestations, he had the animal passions of a strong man'. . . . .

These new personality traits contrasted sharply with the 'temperate habits' and 'considerable energy of character' Phineas Gage was known to have possessed before the accident. He had had 'a well balanced mind and was looked upon by those who knew him as a shrewd smart businessman, very energetic and persistent in executing his plans of action'. There is no doubt that in the context of his job [a railway construction foreman] and time, he was successful. So great was the change in him that friends and acquaintances could hardly recognise the man.[3]

Gage lost his foreman's job, and then became an itinerant worker on horse farms. His quick temper and frequent shows of dissatisfaction got him into trouble, and he drifted from farm to farm. After a brief career as a circus attraction on account of his head wounds, and more farm work both in the United States and in South America, he died a drunken, brawling figure in San Francisco at the age of thirty-eight.

What Damasio finds striking is that brain damage could leave so many motor, language, memory, and attention skills intact and yet destroy important capacities for coping with adult life. As these capacities specifically were taken away as a result of damage to specific parts of the brain, perhaps

something in the brain was concerned specifically with. . . . the ability to anticipate the future and plan accordingly within a complex social environment; the sense of responsibility toward the self and others; and the ability to orchestrate one's survival deliberately at the command of one's free will.[4]

[3] Ibid., p. 8.
[4] Ibid., p. 10.

And perhaps, Damasio conjectured, this something in the brain was also responsible for the component of anticipation and planning that consists of feeling.

In fact, the Gage case is inconsistently described. For while Damasio speaks of the defect in decision making and 'otherwise intact cognition and behaviour',[5] Harlow's eyewitness account refers to Gage's 'intellectual capacities being decidedly impaired, but not totally lost; nothing like dementia, but they were enfeebled in their manifestations'.[6] If cognitive incapacity is mixed up with Gage's bad decision making, the idea of something in the brain responsible for decision making apart from cognition is seriously compromised. In addition to this, however, Damasio seems to tie an extremely complex ability to a certain piece of brain machinery. Nothing less than Gage's respect for social convention, his sense of social responsibility, and his ethics are impaired by his brain injury. There is something odd about mapping a capacity painted in such broad brushstrokes onto, as it turns out, the ventro-medial sector of the brain. Just as the now derided science of phrenology explained the Gage case unsatisfactorily by identifying centres in the brain for benevolence and veneration,[7] and suggesting that the iron bar that had passed between these centres; so it seems wrong to say that respect for social convention and ethics is the work of the ventro-medial sector, or that it is the work of this sector once the appropriate social conditioning has taken place.

The case of 'Elliot' provides far more convincing evidence for Damasio's hypothesis, because the patient was subjected to a very extensive series of psychological tests after surgery, and because the results of these tests put it beyond doubt that Elliot was of above average intelligence. The tests even showed that Elliot had good skills for judging consequences of actions and for making moral judgements in the abstract, though these skills seemed to evaporate when Elliot was faced with the management of his own life. Again, the extent and location of Elliot's brain damage, once his tumour was removed, were known in detail, while the corresponding facts in the case of Gage were not recorded at post mortem, but had to be reconstructed.

---

[5] Ibid., p. 12.
[6] Ibid., quoted on p. 17.
[7] Ibid., p. 17.

After the tumour in his brain was removed,

Elliot was no longer Elliot... He needed prompting to get started in the morning and prepare to go to work. Once at work he was unable to manage his time properly: he could not be trusted to stick to a schedule. When the job called for interrupting an activity and turning to another, he might persist nonetheless, seemingly losing sight of his main goal. Or he might interrupt the activity [in which] he had engaged, to turn to something he found more captivating at that particular moment.... One might say that Elliot had become irrational concerning the larger frame of behaviour, which pertained to his main priority, while within the smaller frames of behaviour which pertained to his subsidiary tasks, his actions were unnecessarily detailed.[8]

In general, Elliot could not be relied upon to finish a task at the time it was supposed to be. He was dismissed from the firm to which he returned after his operation, and he lost many other jobs subsequently. Branching out into business independently, he tried and failed to launch a number of different enterprises and then lost all his money in a partnership with someone he had been strongly advised not to collaborate with. His first marriage failed; then several others. Although apparently able to understand that his decisions were going wrong, he was unable to learn from his mistakes.

Damasio put Elliot through a whole series of tests that might reveal measurable impairment of different cognitive functions, including tests that challenged or defeated patients with frontal lobe brain damage, but Elliot passed them all. In particular he was able to sort cards by rapidly shifting sorting criteria, and he passed subtle tests for arriving at conclusions from scattered background information,[9] for generating alternative responses to different social situations, such as assuaging the anger of someone whose property one damages,[10] and for anticipating consequences in cases where one is tempted to transgress ordinary social conventions (keeping the extra money a bank clerk pays out by mistake). Elliot was able to think up means for attaining a goal arbitrarily specified by experimenters, and he could propose means by which someone might have succeeded in making a

---

[8] Ibid., p. 36.
[9] Ibid., p. 42.
[10] Ibid., p. 47.

range of new friendships.[11] He also did well in a standard test for making moral judgements.[12] Elliot 'passed' in the sense that his responses were not measurably different from those of a control group. In order to identify verifiable abnormality, Damasio and his colleagues had to arrive at new tests. The crucial experiment was one in which Elliot was shown

emotionally-charged visual stimuli – for instance, pictures of buildings collapsing in earthquakes, houses burning, people injured in gory accidents, or about to drown in floods. As we debriefed Elliot from one of the many sessions of viewing these images, he told me without equivocation that his own feelings had changed from before his illness. He could sense how topics that once had evoked a strong emotion no longer caused any reaction, positive or negative.

This was astounding. Try to imagine not feeling pleasure when you contemplate a painting you love or hear a favourite piece of music. Try to imagine yourself forever robbed of that possibility and yet aware of the intellectual contents of the visual or musical stimulus, and also aware that once it did give you pleasure. We might summarize Elliot's predicament as *to know but not to feel.*[13]

'Astounding' seems to overstate what the experiment revealed. After all, 'to know but not to feel' might summarise a form of clinical depression, which is far more common than the tumour apparently at the root of Elliot's problems.

Nevertheless, Elliot's lack of feeling seemed to Damasio to be connected with his lost sense of judgement in day-to-day life:

I began to think that the cold-bloodedness of Elliot's reasoning prevented him from assigning different values to different options, and made his decision-making landscape hopelessly flat. It might also be that the same cold-bloodedness made his mental landscape too shifty and unsustained for the time required to make response selections, in other words, a subtle rather than basic defect in working memory, which might alter the remainder of the reasoning process required for a decision to emerge.[14]

This passage seems to me to identify two quite different effects of cold-bloodedness: on the one hand, the flatness of the landscape – Elliot did

[11] Ibid., p. 47.
[12] Ibid., p. 48.
[13] Ibid., p. 45.
[14] Ibid., p. 51.

not feel strongly enough about many things for his feelings to set up an ordering of preferences, as feelings might in a normal person; on the other hand, the same cold-bloodedness was supposed to contribute to a loss of focus necessary for carrying Elliot from thinking about his options to choosing one and acting. The claim that this second defect was present, though it may be borne out by what Damasio tells us of Elliot's decision-making problems, does not seem at first sight to have much to do with the absence of emotion. As for the first defect, how is the alleged flatness of the emotional landscape to be squared with Elliot's having pursued a variety of business schemes in the first place, or with his having taken a succession of jobs? He must have felt strongly enough about the disastrous enterprise in which he lost all of his money to have ignored the advice against going into it. So was he so cold-blooded after all?

The coherence of Damasio's hypothesis is further thrown into doubt by the claim that the cases of Gage and Eliot are strongly comparable:

In all likelihood the emotional defect was also present in Gage, but the record does not allow us to be certain. We can infer at least that he lacked the feeling of embarrassment, given his use of foul language, and his parading of self-misery.[15]

But Gage was anything but 'cold-blooded' or highly detached, as Elliot was, and the 'parading of self-misery' is hardly compatible with emotionlessness. We also know from passages quoted earlier that Gage was easily made angry. Whatever is to be said about Elliot, the case of Gage seems to be consistent with the traditional view that emotions lead to bad decision making when they get the better of the judgement of consequences and other 'rational' skills. It is true, as Damasio says, that both Gage and Elliot started to make bad decisions after suffering probably similar forms of brain damage: What isn't clear is that the phenomenon of making bad decisions is unitary enough to be a stable explanandum. It might be a bit like 'antisocial' behaviour, which can range from reclusiveness to assault and racialist harassment via drug taking and the casual use of obscenity in conversation. No one would look for a single cause of this behaviour, even if it were found

---

[15] Ibid., p. 51.

that some 'antisocial' people were physiologically similar in some unexpected respect.

Even where defects in decision making are more closely tied to the
absence of emotion than to instability of emotion, so that a clear class
of cases like that of Elliot emerges, it is not obvious that a certain kind
of brain damage accounts for emotionlessness, which in turn accounts
for decision-making problems. It may be that the brain damage causes
emotionlessness and decision-making problems, but not the latter *by
way of* the former. My own view is that the class of cases Damasio constructs[16] does not display enough of a common pattern, and that he
never establishes that brain damage affects decision making by way
of emotional damage.[17] Far from coming up with a 'Phineas Gage
matrix'[18] – a shared essence of syndromes linking many other cases
to Gage's – Damasio seems to me to maintain coherence among very
different cases – those of Gage and Elliot being notable – only by cor-
relating a fairly constant kind of brain damage with a very vaguely
described kind of behavioural failing – bad decision making.

Damasio does better when he puts forward his positive account,[19]
which revolves around what he calls the 'somatic marker hypothesis'.
He breaks down decision making into a process in which practical
options are efficiently narrowed down by the bodily reactions they
evoke. (Damasio is particularly impressed with reactions consisting of
sensing the body frame, heartbeat, and so on and activity at the skin
surfaces.[20]) Not only are felt bodily responses to different images –
somatic markers – necessary to eliminating options in deliberation;
they may be necessary to keeping going or concentrating the attention
and memory processes that precede practical choice.[21]

The brain does not lay out all the possible alternatives and then
arrive by a long process of reasoning and calculation at the one with the
greatest benefit or least cost. Certain options are not even entertained.
Others are entertained only long enough to be rejected, because of

---

[16] Ibid., ch. 4.
[17] This objection applies also to the experiments Damasio describes in Chapter 9 of
Descartes's Error.
[18] Ibid., p. 56.
[19] Ibid., ch. 8.
[20] See ibid., pp. 230ff.
[21] Ibid., pp. 197–8.

the unpleasant feelings they immediately evoke. Symmetrically, some options rise to the top of the pecking order by the gut reactions they cause, rather than by a calculation of their utilities. The medium for the provocation of gut reactions is images that summarise what the agent thinks is at stake in making one choice rather than another. Some gut reactions are widely shared by creatures that can "act" at all, and are not necessarily conscious. They are biologically wired in. These may account for the avoidance of objects in one's path or for avoidance behaviour when we are in the path of something bigger than we are. These may also account for some of the behaviour that attends getting hungry, or escaping a predator.[22] Other gut reactions, according to Damasio, are the accumulated effects of social interaction on a normal brain. In a healthy culture these reactions might include repulsion at the thought of violence or humiliation directed at other people. In a 'sick' culture – Damasio cites the example of Stalinist Russia or the China of the Cultural Revolution – violence and humiliation may feel different.

The somatic marker hypothesis is tied by Damasio to a hypothesis about the system in the brain that handles somatic marker signalling of the wired-in kind, and the more complex decision-making processes involved in planning a long-term business venture or reaching the conclusion that someone should be forgiven. The prefrontal cortices are identified as the part of the brain responsible.[23] The 'entire pre-frontal region seems dedicated to categorising contingencies [that might be considered in practical deliberation] in the perspective of personal relevance.'[24] More specifically,

the bioregulatory and social domains seem to have an affinity for the systems in the ventromedial sector, while systems in the dorsolateral region appear to align themselves with domains which subsume knowledge of the external world (entities such as objects and people, their actions in space-time; language; mathematics; music).

---

[22] Ibid., pp. 167–8. In writings that have come after *Descartes's Error*, Damasio has identified consciousness as a device for maximising in a creature's interests. See *The Feeling of What Happens: Body, Emotion, and the Making of Consciousness* (London: Vintage, 2000), p. 24.

[23] Ibid., pp. 180ff.

[24] Ibid., p. 182.

These hypotheses fit in well with the range of impaired decision making observed in people with damage to different parts of the prefrontal region.

Damasio contrasts the somatic marker hypothesis, which accords such importance to the emotions in decision making, with the 'pure reason' or 'high-reason' view. This is the view that Damasio associates with Descartes and other rationalist philosophers, and the view that he thinks has been appropriated by common sense. According to the 'high-reason' view,

Formal logic will, by itself, get us to the best available solution for any problem. An important aspect of the rationalist conception is that to obtain the best results, emotions must be kept *out*. Rational processing must be unencumbered by passion.

Basically, in the high-reason view, you take the different scenarios apart and to use current managerial parlance you perform a cost/benefit analysis of each of them. Keeping in mind "subjective expected utility," which is the thing you want to maximize, you infer logically what is good and what is bad. For instance, you consider the consequences of each option at different points in the projected future and weigh the ensuing losses and gains. Since most problems have far more than . . . two alternatives, your analysis is anything but easy as you go through your deductions.[25]

If agents went through *all* the alternatives, Damasio goes on to say, they would never succeed in doing appropriate things in the available time. They would end up, like 'Elliot' after his operation, getting lost in the minutiae of projects rather than keeping their eye on the principal goal. They would, like another of Damasio's patients, think aloud for half an hour about the relative merits of two dates for an appointment,[26] rather than make a choice effectively.

The complaint against the 'pure reason' view is not just that it cannot account for what happens when we reach decisions as quickly as we do. It is that, at least in its Cartesian version, as Damasio understands Descartes, the 'high-reason' view entirely excludes what Damasio thinks is the empirically correct answer. It excludes the somatic marker hypothesis because it makes reasoning itself the work of

---

[25] Ibid., p. 171.
[26] Ibid., pp. 193–4.

a faculty of the mind that is entirely divorced from the body.[27] Cues from the body about the relative attractiveness of alternatives are, according to Damasio, crucial to decision making that actually fits into the time available to act and the structure set by main and subsidiary goals. More generally, embodiment is an important condition of mentality and even of a sense of self.[28]

Damasio is wrong about Descartes, and the 'high-reason' view seems to be something of a straw man. Although it is true that for Descartes mind and body are supposed to be very different in nature as substances and conceivable independently of one another, Descartes also thinks, as I have tried to explain in detail, that in human beings the two are united and interact, and that sensations which depend on the body convey information important to survival to the brain. Damasio seems not to see the relation between Descartes's dualism of mind and body and his theory of mind–body union. For mind and body to be metaphysically distinct as kinds of things is not for them to be unable to interact, according to Descartes. Again, although Descartes thinks it is desirable for reason to detach itself from the body for arrival at metaphysical truths, he does not think that the same kind of detachment is desirable or perhaps even possible in the pursuit of practical goals, and the strategies for flourishing in practical life that he sketches in *The Passions of the Soul* and in his correspondence with Princess Elizabeth do not in the least call for a full retreat from the body or the senses. They do call for a detachment from some of the *valuations* of things suggested by the body or the senses, but it is straightforwardly part of Descartes's positive view that the senses and passions are often beneficial. It is true that such things as bias decision for the worse are always derived from the body rather than from the mind, according to Descartes; but this does not mean that whatever the body tells the mind about the world or about the goodness or badness of things in it is always misleading or useless. So passion, sensation, and reason are not necessarily opposed, and conducting oneself rationally as a human being means reconciling oneself to the emotional and sensitive part of one's nature just as much as it means maximising rationality. It can even mean manipulating one's own emotional and sensitive side, for

[27] Ibid., p. 248.
[28] Ibid., pp. 238ff.

example taking drugs that will make one feel nauseated by alcohol in order to break one's alcoholism. A 'pure reason' or 'high-reason' view, then, cannot be a view that confines the influences on action to reason. Not, at least, if the view is Descartes's.

Again, how pure can a 'pure reason' view be, if, as Damasio says, what determines its action is expected subjective utility? Expected subjective utility depends on experience; it is not arrived at apriori, as the conclusions of formal logic are, and its subject matter is neither topic neutral nor divorced from feeling. Subjective utility is often *defined* in terms of feeling, and the gut reactions occasioned by the images one conjures up of different possible practical outcomes are in no way excluded by calculations of utility. So long as the images and the gut reactions encode the relative weightings that more formal paper-and-pencil calculations or computers would arrive at, they might be seen as having the content of such reasoning, much as pain and pleasure can be indicators of what science can independently demonstrate is bad or good for us. Because on Damasio's own showing some somatic markers can work unconsciously, and so independent of any consciously felt indicator of anything, how are they supposed to be distinguishable from a certain kind of cognitive state? And if somatic markers can be cognitive states, why can't their interaction with other states be regarded as a kind of reasoning as opposed to emotional reaction? The supposed distinction between a 'pure reason' view and a view that gives significant weight to emotion goes soft, even when the formulation is taken from Damasio and without reference to Descartes.[29]

There *are* important points of disagreement between Damasio and a rationalist view, a Cartesian view in particular, but they appear to be left out of Damasio's account. The most important of these seems to turn on the recognition of a capacity for reflecting upon and criticising one's emotional reactions. To take an example of Damasio's, suppose that I am trying to decide whether to take a flight along a route where serious storms are predicted, and suppose that, in trying to weigh the risks of flying, I picture myself in the cabin of a plane being bucked by massive turbulence, apparently out of control. Although this image

---

[29] Damasio has refined his views about the nature of the emotions in ways he takes (again questionably in my view) to be in the spirit of Spinoza. See *Looking for Spinoza* (London: Heinemann, 2003).

can terrify me and dispose me to postpone travelling until the weather is better, it can also be the subject of reasoning itself. I can reflect that the bucking airplane seems worse than it is, and that though the turbulence will be unpleasant, planes are designed to cope with it. So my plane will probably be able to cope with it and get me to my destination safely. This reflection can in turn offset the disquiet caused by the image and perhaps enable me to overcome my fears about flying now. To make room for this possibility is not to revert to a 'pure reason' view of decision making, because the role of emotion and even the usefulness of an imagistic medium of practical deliberation are both conceded to the somatic marker thesis. Instead, there is a mixed view of deliberation as involving both reason and emotion.

On the other hand, room is made for the possibility that reasoning can override or counteract the effect of images, so that decision making is not just a matter of doing whatever thing has the strongest positive somatic impact or the weakest negative one. Although Damasio is alive to the way in which decision making as it actually takes place can suffer from various kinds of irrationality and error, he does not discuss the way rational reflection on somatic reactions can counteract them. Descartes's writings about the passions are full of the recognition of this sort of effect. Reason can directly affect deliberation, as when it acts to defuse the somatic impact of an image by supplying countervailing information. It can also indicate how to overcome certain feelings with others: hunger with disgust, fear with shame or mirth, and so on.

One reason why Descartes dwells on the capacity for rational reflection and criticism is that he is concerned to guide agents with normal capacities who want to *perfect* themselves, and behave as they morally ought to, rather than, as with Damasio, to identify mechanisms that make the difference between subnormal and normal decision making. Although the two kinds of interest are not incompatible, they are different. Damasio considers 'ethical behaviour' and the impacts of brain damage on it, but he does not discuss the differences between ethical and normal behaviour and often runs the two together. Descartes, who was always interested in normative questions – in the proper conduct of pure enquiry as much as practical life – never does confuse these with the causes of normal human behaviour, and the sort of emphasis he gives to reason may reflect this interest in norms rather than in causes.

There are at least three ways in which, according to Descartes, reason is required for the conduct of human life. First, it is required for understanding that human beings have a composite nature – that each is a union of mind and body, and that good in life means either good for the body, good for the mind, or good for the two together. Second, reason helps to distinguish apparent goods of body and mind from real goods of body and mind. Third, reason reveals implementable means of improving the body and mind or their union, sometimes by physical interventions and sometimes by self-administered psychological therapy. These uses of reason do not account for all of the goods of body and mind and their union that exist, but they probably do include all those that can reliably be obtained by human effort. It is the third use of reason that connects Descartes's moral philosophy to medicine, and that seems to answer Damasio's charge that Descartes is responsible for the tradition of regarding all disorders as physical, physically treatable.[30] It is the second that connects Cartesian rationalism to the theory of practical reason as a faculty for moral decision and judgement. I now turn to that.

CARTESIAN PRACTICAL REASON

As with innocent Cartesianism about mind and body, innocent Cartesianism about practical reason involves departures from some of Descartes's own ideas. Partly this is because Descartes's views on practical reason are geared to Descartes's dualism. In *The Passions of the Soul,* goods are either goods of body or goods of mind or goods of mind–body union. Goods of the mind are generally regarded by Descartes as the best of the genuine goods, and he thinks it is always the body that is responsible for making questionable goods appear to be genuine. Neither the classification of goods that shadows Descartes's dualism, nor the preference for mental over bodily goods, is very compelling, but there is something right, or at least defensible, about the rationalism in which these claims are embedded.

According to Descartes, the passions help healthy human beings to stay alive and flourish – to persist and flourish as a union of mind and body. Love, hate, desire, joy, and sadness are all ways of protecting

---

[30] Ibid., pp. 254ff.

our embodied minds from harm or for improving our condition even when we are healthy. The pleasure we get from exercise when we are not too unfit, for example, helps to make us stronger and more perfect as embodied beings. On the other hand, while our passions are reasonably accurate guides to what is in general good or bad for us in life, they are not infallible. The cake we cannot resist when it is presented to us for dessert probably stimulates the passion that conduces to our eating enough to stay strong and healthy in a natural environment where food is scarce. This passion is out of its element in the food hall of a shopping mall whose customers are already obese, and yet it can still exercise an influence there. So it can mislead the people in the food hall. The passions can also be bad guides to the relative values of things. Things that are pleasurable because they satisfy a current appetite may lead to an addiction that is extremely debilitating; yet the pleasure can make the thing that produces it seem a far greater good than life without addiction. The lower animals are at the mercy of this misleadingness, according to Descartes, but we are not:

[A]ll the animals devoid of reason conduct their lives simply through bodily movements similar to those which, in our case, usually follow upon the passions which move our soul to consent to such movements. Nevertheless, it is not always good for the passions to function in this way, in so far as there are many things harmful to the body which cause no sadness initially (or even produce joy), and in so far as other things are useful to the body, though at first they are disagreeable. Furthermore, the passions almost always cause the goods they represent, as well as the evils, to appear much greater and more important than they are, thus moving us to pursue the former and flee the latter with more ardour and zeal than is appropriate. (*Passions of the Soul,* § 138 CSM I, 376–7; AT XI 431)

Descartes seems to be right about this. A wild bear drawn to the fast food of campers in a national park will eat as much of it as he can get, even though it is probably as bad for him as it is for people, whereas the campers themselves at least have to ignore nutritional information and doctor's advice to indulge themselves as uninhibitedly as the bears do. The campers can save themselves if they reflect on the nutritional information, and on the relative value of living longer on the one hand and enjoying a helping of fries on the other. As Descartes says, 'We must use experience and reason to distinguish good from evil and to know the true value [of things that appear very good or very evil], so

as not to mistake one for another or rush into anything immoderately'
(ibid.).

The seat of reason – the soul – saves us from the ill effects of automatic passionate behaviour. It enables us to become conscious of a
variety of possible goals and to act on them only if they survive critical reflection. To the extent the body-protecting or body-improving
passions are unquestionably good for us, according to Descartes, it
is the rationally correctible or the rationally corrected such passions.
And even when these passions are functioning under the control of
reason, the goods they promote – like bodily health and longer life or
the ability to act more effectively on the external world – are not to be
compared to the goods of the soul. The reason for this is that almost
all goods – and certainly all of the bodily goods – are only contingently
pursuable and gettable. There is nothing in the nature of those goods
to prevent their being unattainable, and they can regularly be out of
our reach. Even when it is in principle in our power to get these goods,
our efforts may come to nothing. The great contingency of many of
the things we pursue may suggest a goal or goals very different from
the ones most people pursue at the instigation of the passions. The
best thing for us to do may be to get very clear on our limitations and
to devote ourselves to the identification and willing of those genuine
good things there can never be a reason for not pursuing.

This strategy is sketched by Descartes in a letter of November 1647
to Queen Christina of Sweden. Descartes is considering a traditional
question in moral philosophy – that of what good in life is the 'highest'
or 'greatest': the one that organises all or other goals, but that itself is
not subordinate to further goals:

In trying to decide this question, my first observation is that we should not
consider anything as good, in relation to ourselves, unless we either possess
it or have the power to acquire it. Once this is agreed, it seems to me that
the supreme good of all men together is the total or aggregate of all of the
goods – those of the soul and the body and of fortune – which can belong
to any human being; but that the supreme good of each individual is quite a
different thing, and consists only of a firm will to do well and the contentment
which this produces. My reason for saying this is that I can discover no other
good which seems so great or so entirely within each man's power. For the
goods of the body and of fortune do not depend entirely on us; and those
of the soul can be reduced to two heads, the one being to know, and the

other to will, what is good. But knowledge is often beyond our powers; and so there remains only our will, which is absolutely within our disposal. And I do not see that it is possible to dispose it better than by a firm and constant resolution to carry out to the letter all things which one judges to be best, and to employ all the powers of one's mind in finding out what these are. This by itself constitutes the virtues; this alone really deserves praise and glory; this alone, finally, produces the greatest and most solid enjoyment in life. (CSM III 324–5; AT V 82–3)

He is saying that the best thing in life is willing what we have rationally concluded is the best thing to do. This general goal leaves nothing to chance. Not only can it never be beyond us to will what we carefully conclude it's best to do; we never have reason to think we should have done something else. It can never be beyond us to do our best; and having done our best, there is nothing else there was better reason for us to do and in our power; otherwise, it wouldn't have been our *best* that we did; or our concluding that a certain thing was best to do was not careful enough; and what is at issue is the status of resolutions based on the most careful consideration possible for us.

Descartes admits that even when we have done our utmost to figure out the right thing to do, and even when we have tried our hardest to do that thing, it can still turn out that what we do is bad (ibid. AT V 84). But he denies that what turns out badly when we have done our best in the required way is material for regret. So far as what was known and in his power is concerned, the agent did nothing wrong. In a clear sense for Descartes there are things that turn out badly that an agent *should* have done, and what is bad about the outcome does not reflect badly on the agent. What reflects badly on an agent is doing what turns out to be the right thing, though the agent judges it isn't. For then the agent had reason not to do it or to do something else, and yet did it anyway (ibid.). Relative to the deliberation that led up to it, the action is reckless or wrong, and it should seem that way to the agent. When it is judged to be contrary to reason, it will also *feel* wrong. It will give rise to displeasure or disturbance in the deliberator. Doing one's best and knowing as much, on the other hand, always produces pleasure, and particularly solid pleasure at that. It is solid because, compared with other goods than those of carrying out a well-judged resolution, one can reflect that everything in carrying out that resolution is due to the agent. In the case of other actions, even those carried out for one's health or protection, many of the things that need to happen or to exist for one's action to succeed lie outside one's will. So there is a limit to the pleasure one can take in those actions. In protecting oneself from an attacker's blow, for example, one needs to have good reflexes, but whether one has good reflexes does not depend on one's will. So it is not entirely clear that the pleasure of successfully defending oneself is justified by what one *does*. By contrast, carrying out the general resolution to try one's hardest to do what one thinks is best does not involve working parts that are external to the will. It is wholly inalienable. Or as Descartes says in the same letter to Queen Christina quoted earlier, 'There is nothing that is more our own than the [free] will' (CSM III 326; AT V 85). The correct disposition of the will, then, deserves all the credit it attracts, including the pleasure the agent feels in what he has done or decided to do.

Now a fully informed free will is going to have very different plans from a wild bear, or from a rational but not fully informed human being. The fully informed free will can pursue only what it is sure are genuine goods, which means resisting or ignoring the promptings of many appetites that bring with them distorted valuations. The fully informed free will will also probably aim at projects of self-reform – those that depend maximally on the will – rather than at projects of changing radically either nature or society, which require the concurrence of things independent of one's own will. More specifically, the fully informed free will can be expected to work at eliminating, or reducing the influence of, what Descartes calls the 'less useful desires' (CSM I 379; AT XI 437). These are desires for things that do not depend solely on us, or desires that, though they are in our power to satisfy, agitate the animal spirits in ways that are bad for bodily health. In practice, counteracting the less useful desires will be a matter of cultivating both a certain sort of fatalism about outcomes of choice, and a kind of inwardness. Our responsibility extends only to reaching decisions about what to do; implementing those decisions means inserting our chosen outcomes into the order of events decided by God.

Whether the insertion is successful is a matter of whether God has left a space for the implementation of our choice in natural history – in the history of the external world. He may very well not have. So we may be conscientious but ineffectual. Where the implementation of our choices appears *not* to be precarious is in the area of what Descartes calls "internal emotions" – feelings produced by and in the soul as a result of doing one's best to do what one has scrupulously chosen. Descartes seems to have in mind the satisfactions of conscientiousness, which he thinks are always accessible to us and impervious to fortune (CSM I, 381–2; AT XI 441–2). So the key to well-being – the main precept of practical reason – is to decide as carefully as one can, in the light of as accurate as possible a view of the goods of mind and body, and implement the decision as wholeheartedly as one can.

There is a characteristically Cartesian tinge to the division of human goods into the goods of mind and body. There is also a characteristically Cartesian bias in the background rankings of the goods that are supposed to guide choice, a bias against the body and in favour of the soul. The body is the source of everything in us that opposes reason (CSM I 346; AT XI 365); it is the 'lesser part' of us, in comparison to the soul (CSM I 377; AT XI 432); and if we had no body, 'we could not go too far in abandoning ourselves to love and joy, and in avoiding hatred and sadness' (CSM I 378; AT XI 434). Just as it is the soul, or the soul's faculty of reason, that enables it to know a reality that the senses distort, a reality built systematically out of the simple natures of the mental and the physical; so it is the soul and its faculty of reason that enables the human being to see what is good other than through the distorting lens of bodily appetite. Though the bodily appetites are good as rough guides to what to pursue and avoid, they cannot point the way to the best kind of human well-being, for that does not seem to depend on embodiment at all. The best kind of human well-being is the kind that cannot be spoiled by how things happen to turn out. This bias against the body is not the bias Damasio claims to identify. Descartes can accommodate somatic signalling in an account of how ordinary or normal practical deliberation takes place, and he does not think information from and about the body has no place in an account of any kind of human well-being. It is the *highest* sort of well-being that seems to bypass the body, according to Descartes. And the problem with this sort of well-being is that it does not seem to be a human well-being – a well-being of the embodied soul, as opposed to a well-being of the soul. It is as if to live best, human beings have to identify with what is spiritual in them or rational in them, rather than what depends on being alive.

INNOCENT CARTESIANISM ABOUT PRACTICAL REASON

I do not believe that an innocent Cartesianism can display ambivalence about the humanity of agents, or incorporate a strong dualism of goods of the body and goods of the soul. But to say this is not to call into question Descartes's rationalism about action. In other words, Descartes seems to me to be right to claim that some apparent goods are illusory, that we can rationally discover as much, and that we can act accordingly. Descartes seems right to claim further that the identification of genuine goods seems to depend on knowledge of the nature of human beings, and not just a matter of being guided by what feels good. This is where the perfections of mind and body come in. Knowing what is good for the body and soul is a matter partly of knowing what an ideal body or soul is like, and this is a task of reason or conceptual thought, rather than experience. Perhaps it is partly an apriori or metaphysical task, because not everything about us – not everything about the mind – is aposteriori knowable or understandable as the effect of matter in motion.

This much seems to be right even if goods in general do not divide into goods of the body and goods of the soul, and even if goods of the soul are not always superior to goods of the body. For example, it may be right to say that health is a genuine good, even if health is not just a good of the body. Again, it might be right to say that the pleasure of taking very addictive drugs is illusory, even if the addictive drug heightens one's intellectual powers, and gives intellectual pleasure, which is high in Descartes's hierarchy of goods. It might be right to say that the genuineness of the good of health is a reason for an agent to look after his own health, even if he does not care about his health. Further, it seems right to say that some capacity for monitoring and thinking about one's appetites and the consequences of indulging them is essential to a full-blooded human well-being, even if the monitoring is the work of the brain rather than the soul. It seems right to say that these capacities for reflection and monitoring sometimes weaken the very appetites and desires they are directed upon, and so increase the autonomy of the agent, even if the subject of that autonomy is not a Cartesian soul. And there is something right about trying to identify a general form of moral precept that ensures the coordination of 'ought' and 'can' while preserving a source of exactingness and inescapability. In Descartes, the practical precept is to the effect that one should decide carefully what is best to do (in the light of the perfections minds and bodies are capable of) and do one's utmost to implement one's choice. Everyone has an incentive to do this, because it gives a sure and solid well-being; and no one can fail to be able to do this because, necessarily, everyone can do their best. So everyone has a reason to do it and no one has a reason not to (inescapability).

It pulls together these strands of innocent Cartesianism about practical reason to focus on two of its elements: the thesis that something is genuinely good only if it helps to perfect an agent, and the thesis that the successful pursuit of the good is a matter of what one wills rather than what one actually brings about. The first thesis expresses philosophical realism about goods or about what improves us. What is good for us is logically independent of what merely feels good to us, and what is bad for us is similarly independent of what feels bad. What is good for us as embodied beings is whatever – independently of feeling – preserves or improves bodily functioning, and what is good for us as souls or minds is whatever – independent of the pleasure it produces – improves our capacity for knowing and willing the good. This realism about goods or sources of improvement can also be expressed as a version of "externalism" about reasons: External reasons are reasons for agents not actually motivated to do a thing, to do it. The fact that an action would contribute to what is objectively an improvement – a gain in physical strength, for example – is a reason for an agent to do it, even if he does not care about being strong or getting stronger.[31] Indeed, it is not just a reason but a *good* reason to do it, so that the agent acts irrationally, and hence wrongly from a Cartesian point of view, if he ignores it when there is no better reason (understood again in terms of the perfections) for doing something else.

Both the philosophical realism and the externalism of the Cartesian position seem to me to be correct or at least defensible. To begin with the relevant form of realism, it seems clear on the strength of examples already drawn from Descartes's writings that pleasure is neither necessary nor sufficient for bodily improvement, and it seems clear

---

[31] The term 'external reason' is Bernard Williams's. See his 'Internal and external reasons' reprinted in *Moral Luck* (Cambridge: Cambridge University Press, 1981), pp. 101–13. Williams is sceptical about the existence of external reasons.

that various kinds of unpleasantness may be involved in intellectual or moral improvement. To cite one of a range of examples that could be used, gaining the capacity to read or speak a new language is clearly an enlargement of an intellectual capacity, but both the acquisition and retention of linguistic skills can involve tedious drills. Very similar considerations apply in the case of the acquisition of mathematical skills. And perhaps the getting of moral wisdom is no picnic either, though it does us much good. The Cartesian position probably extends to saying that certain forms of human improvement and deterioration are genuine not only independent of pleasantness or unpleasantness, but independent of what is widely believed in the society of the relevant people. Cases of bodily improvement or deterioration already cited support this view, even if it is conceded that the conditions for regaining health and so for some kinds of human improvement are not always a matter simply of *bodily* improvement.

Externalism about reasons is a more disputable matter, perhaps. Apart from the arguments in favour of internalism – that is, in favour of the view that the only reasons there are for an agent to do things are reasons that are operative in the agent and that could in principle explain something he did, there are arguments which say that the distinction between internal and external reasons is questionable.[32] I believe that internalism must be wrong as a thesis about agents who are able critically to reflect on their plans or intentions; for if such critical reflection is to make sense at all, it must be able to be characterised as a process of trying to discover external reasons – reasons the agent does not yet have, but that a person might have, or that other sensible people are known to have – for doing or omitting something the agent is thinking of doing. The general form of question lying behind this critical reflection must be, 'Is there a (good) reason for or against X'; not, 'Is there some reason among the reasons I already have for doing or not doing X?' as if the point were to dredge up unconscious but operative reasons, or as if the point were to give more weight to an operative reason that had not yet been given sufficient weight.

Again, there is something about Descartes's candidates for things there are external reasons to do – things that improve bodily

---

[32] See Christine Korsgaard, 'Scepticism about Practical Reason', *Journal of Philosophy* 83 (1986), pp. 5–25; see also the title essay of J. David Velleman, *The Possibility of Practical Reason* (Oxford: Oxford University Press, 2000) pp. 170–99.

functioning or that protect an agent's life – that may make all agents who are able to reflect rationally and critically on their plans reasonably receptive to them. There is the fact that many of these reasons, if acted upon, enlarge the range of options an agent has and need not use up opportunities that come only once. Someone who gives weight to his own preservation is extending his term as agent and so has more opportunities than an agent who is equally capable but lives less time. Someone who increases his physical power is able to enlarge the repertoire of things he deliberates about to include feats of strength, without necessarily losing any options. An agent for whom feats of strength are not an option is in a sense worse off. The option-increasing aspect of some of the things that there are external reasons for doing, as well as the compatibility of many of these things with an agent's existing projects, may make them cost-free or even wholly advantageous, which raises the question of whether they wouldn't be internalised if the agent became aware of them. How can an agent not be receptive to a thing that leaves all his other options intact? Another route to receptiveness to Descartes's candidates for external reasons is the agent's consciousness of his humanity and his access to the idea that there are things that are good for humans – indeed, needed by humans if they are to live. How can an agent accept that there are such things as human needs, recognise that *he* is human, and still not have a reason to make sure that he gets or does what will satisfy those needs?

Externalism seems initially plausible in proportion to the degree of consistency of would-be external reasons with other reasons, and in proportion to the generality of facts about agents that they engage with. People who are genuinely hungry need to eat and so there is an external reason for them to be fed, or for anyone to feed them or give money for a famine-relief agency to do so. Perhaps, however, when would-be external reasons try to reach into the detail of people's lives by considerations more specific than the requirements of human survival or moderate well-being, they overreach themselves. Sometimes this seems to be the upshot of internalist arguments. Williams gives the example of someone who

(I use 'ought' in an unspecific way here) ought to be nicer to his wife. I say, 'You have a reason to be nicer to her'. He says, 'What reason?' I say, 'Because she is your wife'. He says – and he is a very hard case – 'I don't care. Don't you understand? I really do not care'. I try various things on him, and try to involve him in this business; and I find that he really is a hard case; there is *nothing* in his motivational set that gives him a reason to be nicer to his wife as things are.

There are many things I can say about or to this man: that he is ungrateful, inconsiderate, hard, sexist, nasty, brutal, and many other disadvantageous things. I shall presumably say, whatever else I say, that it would be better if he were nicer to her. There is one specific thing that the external reasons theorist wants me to say, that the man has a reason to be nicer. . . . What is supposed to make [this form of words] appropriate, as opposed to (or in addition to) all those other things that may be said?[33]

I do not see why the case of the man who sees no reason why he should be nicer to his wife is different from the case of someone who sees no reason why he should stop taking heroin. Even if it is not addiction speaking through him, even if all things considered he soberly endorses his use of heroin, the effects of heroin give a reason why he shouldn't take it. And the damage done to the wife implied by her being the object of brutal, selfish, or sexist treatment similarly gives a reason why it shouldn't be done to her. This same damage may be the ground of what Williams seems to think is the less philosophically loaded thought that it would be better if the husband were nicer to her. But surely what makes it better for the husband to be nicer is whatever is damaging about the current state of things, and to say it's damaging is to say that *ceteris paribus* there is a reason not to do it. If this line of thought is correct, there may be external reasons at a high level of generality *and* external reasons at the level of life's fine detail.

Earlier I distinguished two unifying theses of innocent Cartesianism about practical reason. One was that something is genuinely good only if it helps to perfect an agent. The second thesis is that the successful pursuit of the good is a matter of what one wills rather than what one actually brings about. In Descartes, this thesis is allied to a metaphysics which implies that much more is beyond human control than we like to think. As soon as decision translates into muscular contraction and bodily movement, it does so only because a god who has power over everything (even the so-called necessary truths) permits it to. And so actions are not entirely ours. Our genuine sphere of

---

[33] 'Internal Reasons and the Obscurity of Blame' in Bernard Williams, *Making Sense of Humanity* (Cambridge: Cambridge University Press, 1995), p. 39.

influence begins and ends with the scope we have for disposing the will. Because Descartes's views about God's omnipotence have long struck many commentators as suspect, how far can his picture of where practical reasoning ends up be accepted? And if he might be wrong about what we are responsible for, how innocent a Cartesianism can it be that holds that disposing our will is all that matters morally?

In order to move unreconstructed Cartesianism about the will in the direction of innocent Cartesianism, we need to substitute for Descartes's identification of the will with the spiritual self, the identification of the will with certain second-order desires of the human being. There is an unreconstructed Cartesian interpretation of what it is for an agent to own a choice, and also an innocent Cartesian interpretation. The unreconstructed interpretation homes in on the bit of inner space that is constituted by well-grounded practical judgements. These are wholly formed by oneself and are therefore one's own. They are also exercises of the one thing that we earlier saw Descartes tell Queen Christina was more our own than anything else – the free will. But exercising the free will is not necessarily acting in the sense of producing bodily movements. External or internal things can intervene. This fact, as we saw earlier, shrinks the sphere of autonomous action to rational practical judgement one *tries* to act upon. So we can say that in unreconstructed Cartesianism a choice is owned when its source is a well-grounded judgement of the soul, and when that judgement leads to effort in accordance with it. Unreconstructed Cartesianism also calls on agents to tailor their practical judgements to what they have control over. This is mainly our psychological attitudes, rather than what happens outside us or what we might try to do to change the world for our benefit.

Innocent Cartesianism, on the other hand, identifies the will with an agent's attitude to the desires he acts upon. It has nothing much to do with Stoicism or fatalism. Compared with unreconstructed Cartesianism, it has a higher standard of what it is for an agent to follow through with one's practical judgements. It looks to action rather than mere effort, and it allows agents to be held responsible, and to hold themselves responsible, for bad things they do but do unwillingly in a certain sense. These are things agents can regret and have reason to regret, even though in a certain sense it was not their will that the regretted actions be done. So innocent Cartesianism undoes Descartes's idea that the only object of regret is less than full effort in the service of some rationally arrived at objective.

The framework for an innocent Cartesianism about the will is present, I think, in Harry Frankfurt's classic paper 'Freedom of the Will and the Concept of a Person'.[34] Although Frankfurt is a Descartes scholar, he does not himself associate the proposal in his article with Cartesianism. Frankfurt's thesis is that the concept of a person applies only to subjects who, in addition to being agents, care about what they want. He thinks most or all nonhuman animals count as nonpersons according to this criterion, as do young children. For although all can act on first-order desires, none can do so reflectively. Even some sane adult human beings fail Frankfurt's test of personhood. They are "wantons" – subjects who have various first-order desires, but no de-sires that any of these first-order desires should 'be their will' or be implemented. Wantons act according to whichever first order desires turn out to be the strongest, and it does not matter to them that one rather than another of these prevails. Wantons in Frankfurt's sense in-clude nonhuman animals as Descartes understands them – creatures that automatically do whatever it is their strongest desires impel them to do. But wantons can also have the capacity to deliberate and choose the moment on which they act on their strongest desire. They need not translate their strongest desires into action heedlessly or at once.[35]

Persons in Frankfurt's sense can act on first-order desires that they not only do not want to be their will, but that they fight against. The un-willing drug addict is a person of this kind. For though he takes drugs, he wishes he didn't, and he wants not to have the wants that lead him to do it. Frankfurt takes it that second-order desires arise as part of rational reflection, and so they are not mere passions in Descartes's sense. Again, they play the role that 'the will' plays in Descartes. For they are reasons for action that reason recommends. But the fact that these second-order volitions are ineffectual and the agent acts con-trary to them – these facts get weight as well in Frankfurt, whereas in Descartes they do not. In Frankfurt's framework, as far as I can see, the fact that the drug addict has tried but failed does not make regret

---

[34] Reprinted in Frankfurt's *The Importance of What We Care About* (Cambridge: Cambridge University Press, 1998).
[35] Ibid., p. 17.

inappropriate; but in Descartes the failing is inevitable and beyond the agent's control. In Frankfurt the freedom to act is much more widely available than the freedom of the will. Freedom to act is the freedom to realise first-order desires in action. An addict has this freedom, though it may take the form of handcuffing himself, or admitting himself into a treatment centre where people will prevent his taking drugs. So if he fails to stop taking drugs or to stop himself taking drugs, this can be a matter for regret. But there can still be a sense in which he takes drugs against his will and so in that sense unfreely; for the first-order desire he acts in accordance with conflicts with what he wants his will to be. The point is that this sense of unfreedom does not deprive regret of application.

Though the move in the direction of Frankfurt takes Cartesianism into the sphere of action, and extends the scope for rational regret, it does not deprive the notion of the will of any use, or even undercut the claim that the will is more of a true possession of the subject than anything else. In a sense this remains true in Frankfurt's framework, for it is through second-order volitions that a subject stamps his identity on actions, and it is important that second-order volitions seem to be formed from a position of detachment from unwilled appetites or sensations and the adventitious generally.[36] The volitions come from somewhere deep in the self and are not by-products of its interplay with anything else. So in a sense they are deeply ours. But because they are also supposed to be in conformity to reason, and so presumably in keeping with what it is rational to think is good for the mind or body, second-order volitions are not necessarily individual or distinctive. They are deeply expressive of a self, but perhaps it is a self available to everyone, like the 'I' of the *Meditations*.

---

[36] For the importance of the difference between what Frankfurt calls volitions and appetites, see Gary Watson's development of the distinction between desires and valuations – judgements of the good. In 'Free Agency' reprinted in G. Watson, ed., *Free Will* (Oxford: Oxford University Press, 1982), pp. 96–110. Watson thinks that the role played by some of Frankfurt's second-order volitions (to indicate the agent's will) is in fact played by (first-order) judgements of the good (p. 109). Watson thinks that the underlying position in Frankfurt – as well as his own – is Platonic, but he could have said, with equal justice, Cartesian.

6

Anthropology, Misogyny, and Anthropocentrism

In Descartes, the soul or mind is complete on its own; the embodied mind or human being, though it forms a kind of unity, is a secondary and metaphysically inferior kind of thing. Finite souls or minds can conceivably exist not only in the absence of human beings but in the absence of all bodies; on the other hand, there is no such thing as a human being without a mind, at least as Descartes understands human beings. What is more, normal human beings are only temporary unities of minds and bodies; when death occurs, the body disintegrates, ceases to function, and loses its connection with the soul; but the soul loses only its powers of sensation and imagination and some of the emotions. These are no real loss, according to Descartes, because within the soul not all capacities are on a level. Reason and understanding are essential in ways that perception and imagination, pleasure, pain, and many other emotions are not. The soul or mind not only stands above what is human in a certain sense: It stands apart from everything that is animal. Nonhuman animals have some sort of inner life, at least as I read Descartes; but it largely consists of sensation, which is one of those capacities a soul can lack while remaining a soul.

Many critics of Descartes cite these claims about what is essential and inessential as evidence of a double prejudice: a prejudice in favour of the human and against the rest of nature, and a prejudice in favour of reason and against everything else in the realm of mental. This latter prejudice the critics connect with a bias toward what is male. Though they are not entirely baseless, such misgivings about Descartes's own ideas are hard to make precise or compelling. And as we have discovered in connection with other topics, there may be the makings of an innocent Cartesianism even in highly rationalistic and dualistic views of human beings. In this chapter, the possibilities of innocent Cartesianism are indicated in relation to gender, the animal world, and nature more generally. It might be thought that in this connection one would have to depart radically from the unreconstructed Cartesianism of Descartes himself to arrive at a defensible view. Perhaps surprisingly, that isn't so. Unreconstructed Cartesianism is much closer to innocence than it at first appears to be, and it is the critics' misreading that makes it appear otherwise.

CARTESIAN MISOGYNY?

What is there in the idea that when Descartes talks about reason's being the better part of human beings, he is exalting the masculine? A number of feminist writers believe that there is a misogynist subtext to the *Meditations*, and that the valuations implicit in Descartes have seeped into most of the thought affected by the Enlightenment. Before considering the prospects of an innocent Cartesianism in this connection, it may help briefly to consider what is supposed to be lurking between the lines of Descartes's own writings.

A feminist study of the history of philosophy that acknowledges the importance of Descartes is Genevieve Lloyd's pointedly titled *The Man of Reason*.[1] Lloyd argues that while elements of Descartes's theory of reason are egalitarian and in principle neutral between the sexes, others are not. In particular, the association of Descartes's theory of reason with his dualism, and the pride of place he gives, among the applications of reason, to metaphysics as opposed to experimental science and practical pursuits, reinforce a system of intellectual and other roles that make women second-class citizens – second-class citizens of the republic of letters as well as of the wider society. Because it otherwise has egalitarian implications, Descartes's theory may give unintended support to this system of roles, according to Lloyd, but it does reinforce it all the same.

---

[1] G. Lloyd, *The Man of Reason: 'Male and Female' in Western Philosophy* (London: Routledge, 1984), second edition 1993.

Lloyd identifies two aspects of the theory of reason that give it an egalitarian character. First, as she understands Descartes, reason is in a certain sense acquired. It results when method guides thought. It is not a faculty distributed by nature, still less a faculty distributed by nature exclusively or mainly to men. Second, it can be acquired independently of a prevailing education system and may even work better outside such a system, because, in Descartes's view, a curriculum – the scholastic one, for example – can corrupt the intellect. So people excluded from the education system – young women in Descartes's day – are not necessarily at a disadvantage when it comes to developing and applying reason. On the other hand,

There are aspects of Descartes's thought which – however unintentionally – provided a basis for a sexual division of mental labour whose influence is still very much with us. Descartes's emphasis on the equality of Reason has had less influence than his formative contribution to the ideal of a distinctive kind of Reason – a highly abstract mode of thought, separable, in principle, from the emotional complexities and practical demands of ordinary life. . . . We owe to Descartes an influential and pervasive theory of mind, which provides support for a powerful version of the sexual division of mental labour. Women have been assigned responsibility for that realm of the sensuous which the Cartesian Man of Reason must transcend, if he is to have true knowledge of things . . . If he is to exercise the most exalted form of Reason, he must leave soft emotions and sensuousness behind; woman will keep them intact for him.[2]

Although one can see what she means, Lloyd does not really show that the rational Cartesian subject is supposed to be a man. The subject of the most abstract sort of thought is only incidentally embodied, and the soul has no sex. This makes it tendentious to speak of a Cartesian man of reason.

Again, as we saw in the previous chapter, Descartes does *not* think that sensuous and practical human life can dispense with reason, that the application of reason to the pursuit of the good is unimportant, or that practical and sensuous life takes second place to the life of abstract reasoning or speculation. Lloyd recognises some of this, for she is aware of passages in which Descartes says that it is bad for people

[2] Ibid., pp. 49–50.

to devote more than a fraction of their time to metaphysics,[3] but she does not give the line of thought that these passages express the weight it deserves. The quest for metaphysical certainty that dominates the *Meditations* was always distinguished by Descartes from a quest for practical certainty – what he called moral certainty. Achieving metaphysical certainty was a matter of *suspending* daily practical life with its moral certainty and withdrawing – at most once in a lifetime – for a period of deep reflection on the topics of the *Meditations on First Philosophy*. Once those reflections were successfully concluded, the enquirer would be immunised forever more from the doubt that arises when one asks whether one might be of such a nature as to be deceived about what seems most evident (cf. CSM III 228, 346). At that point, according to Descartes, the enquirer could resume the life of the nonparanoid scientist – that is, the life of an inferrer of at most morally certain mechanistic explanations of the behaviour of light, meteorological phenomena, animals, minerals, and the planets. Descartes's nonparanoid scientist, a scientist entirely immunised to the worry that his mind might be defective in nature, is not the same as an unselfconscious craftsman, wholly absorbed through his activity in the world; but neither is the nonparanoid scientist the same as the radically detached self that emerges at the end of Meditation One – disembodied, out of time, out of life, and out of nature. According to Descartes, this metaphysical self and its preoccupations were to be abandoned for good, once one had learned the lesson of the *Meditations*. He did not regard it as an ideal human self, or its preoccupations as the right things to occupy the human mind.

It is with the nonparanoid scientist, the man busy with dissections of animals or busy with instrument making, that the full-time permanent metaphysical enquirer is unfavourably compared by Descartes. Metaphysical enquiry ought to be a full-time occupation for only a short period away from practical scientific life, and it should never be carried out for its own sake, but only to ensure against the subversion of practical scientific life. Metaphysics, then, however foundational, is

---

[3] Lloyd cites the letter to Elizabeth 28 June 1643 (CSM III 227; AT III 692). There are parallel passages in the *Conversation with Burman*, J. Cottingham, ed. and trans. (Oxford: Clarendon Press, 1976), cf. e.g. p. 30.

not the high point of science but rather a taxing preliminary to its main business – physics – which is itself a step on the way towards the most beneficial sciences – morals, mechanics, and medicine, the sciences that change ourselves and the world for human benefit.

It is these beneficial sciences, the fruit-bearing branches of Descartes's tree of science, that are the acme of science, not its metaphysical roots below ground. And of the beneficial sciences it is morals that reigns supreme. As Descartes says in the preface to the French edition of the *Principles*, morals is 'the ultimate level of wisdom'. This science, of course, is for governing action quite generally. It is a science for life, life including natural science, but also extending beyond it. It is a science for making choices in the light of a scale of perfections, rather than for making hedonism efficient. And it classifies and gives strategies for cultivating virtues that are moral and social, not just those that are useful to pursuing the life of the mind. Although this science is the furthest removed from metaphysics in Descartes's scheme of the sciences, it is this as much as physics for which Descartes is laying foundations. The certainty of nonparanoid science; the reliability of elevated moral choice – in a word, rational practical life – is what detached, disembodied, solitary metaphysical reflection paves the way for, and gets its value from. Descartes's rational practical life is not the unselfconscious absorbed activity of a contented craftsman, but neither is it detached, alienated, and stripped of the affective or the passionate. And it is valued higher by Descartes than the intense life of the mind that becomes available with detachment from the senses. That is why the science of it is put above that of metaphysics.

Now it may be true, and it counts in favour of Lloyd's interpretation, that two of the superior Cartesian sciences – medicine and mechanics – were in practice closed off to women in the seventeenth century. But the third, and the science that Descartes placed above all the others, was surely open to everyone. Women were the first students of his moral philosophy, and the most active of the critics who made him refine it. And while it is true that they were noblewomen and sometimes royalty, it is also true that at this level the usual differentiation of intellectual labour between men and women could lapse. Where it did, Descartes's general philosophy gave support to its lapsing: it did not imply that morals *or* metaphysics was no business of women.

Lloyd's argument, then, is at best inconclusive. Susan Bordo is another feminist commentator on Descartes and Cartesianism.[4] Her claim[5] is that in Descartes's hands both nature itself and knowledge of nature are reconceptualised in ways that take away or deny the feminine. Descartes's nature is not a mother nature or even a nature containing feminine elements as well as masculine ones. For example, it is without a passive feminine receptacle for the activity of other natural forces that were traditionally mythologised as male. Instead, Cartesian nature is utterly drained of femininity. What is left – inert and mechanical – is a nature seen through male eyes. Once this image of nature came into its own, there was a corresponding shift, according to Bordo, in the understanding of the right resources for understanding nature. Where previously understanding nature had had to do with sympathy with nature, in Decartes and those of his successors influenced by him, correct understanding turned into a matter of detachment – a matter of subtracting what is subjective from our interactions with nature. This is what she calls the 'Cartesian masculinization' of thought. In general,

[t]he project that fell to both empirical science and 'rationalism' [in the seventeenth century] was to tame the female universe. Empirical science did this through aggressive assault and violation of her 'secrets'. Rationalism . . . tamed the female universe through the philosophical neutralisation of her vitality. The barrenness of matter correlatively insured the revitalization of human hope of conquering nature (through knowledge, in this case, rather than through force).[6]

The answer to Cartesianism, Bordo goes on to say, is the reinstatement of feminine modes of understanding in the public scientific arena. The public scientific arena, rather than some lesser, outlying forum that a male intellectual order is prepared to tolerate as long as it stays at the fringes of cultural activity. She is as strongly opposed to the recognition of an outlying domain of legitimate female understanding

---

[4] S. Bordo, *The Flight to Objectivity: Essays in Cartesianism and Culture* (Albany, N.Y.: SUNY Press, 1987).
[5] Ibid. ch. 6.
[6] Ibid., p. 112.

as she is opposed to the total ouster of female forms of understanding from intellectual life.[7]

Bordo does not explain what natural science would be like if a female sensibility were reinstated, and though she speaks of a reaction against Cartesianism in intellectual life, her examples are drawn exclusively from philosophy and the social sciences:

> Fuelled by the historicist tradition in epistemology, psychoanalytic thought, *and* the political movement for women's rights, representation and participation in cultural life, feminist ethics and epistemology now appears as one of the most vital forces in the development of the post-Cartesian focus and paradigm.[8]

It is unclear how this development is supposed to reorient the understanding of nature that she objects to: To do that, it would have to affect mainstream science, to which femininst epistemology and history of science do not even appear to be addressed. More, the movement Bordo describes seems that of a minority even within philosophy and social sciences.

What about Bordo's account of the Cartesian turn in the study of nature? One difficulty with it is its tendency to conflate nature and matter. It is not true that Descartes turns all of *nature* into inert and dead mechanism; human beings are part of nature, and they contain active principles – wills – that are neither tamed by matter nor explicable as varieties of extension in motion. Again, not every detached view is a detached view of lifeless or inactive nature: For example, it is a detached view of human beings that makes them out as unions of distinct substances, but the relevant detachment – metaphysical detachment – brings into view a genuinely active principle – the will – in human beings. As for whether the Cartesian view suppresses what previous views had acknowledged was feminine in nature, this, too, seems questionable. Cartesianism is certainly directed against an Aristotelian physics, biology, and theory of perception which implied that qualities human beings experienced substances as having were objectively *in* the substances, and that forms conveyed to the mind from that experience were essential to those substances; but this view does not

[7] Ibid., p. 114.
[8] Ibid., p. 115.

seem to be any more feminine than what supersedes it, and though there is a familiar rhetoric against Cartesianism to the effect that its reduction of a lot of nature to matter in motion helped to legitimise any amount of human (and primarily male human) domination and exploitation of nature,[9] the view superseded by Cartesianism was probably even more objectionable.

First, Aristotelianism put the earth at the centre of the universe and anchored the most fundamental explanatory apparatus of physics – the qualities that were used to define the four terrestrial elements – to the human perceptual apparatus. The strong implication is that the universe is intelligible only to humans or creatures perceptually constituted like human beings. Another strong implication is that the explanatory principles of nature leap to the human eye or other sensory organs – that they are on the surface of substances, or at least readily accessible to the senses. In other words, the universe is centred on us humans and peculiarly open to our inspection. By contrast, Cartesianism makes available a picture of the universe in which human beings have no special insight and no special place or status. The Earth is one planet among others; human beings are not necessarily the only intelligent creatures on Earth; there might be others elsewhere; there are certainly intelligences greater than ours – the intelligences of angels and God, to name two. These elements of an intellectual humility are asserted against an Aristotelian physics and biology which said outright that the best in human beings was male, and that helped to support a politics in which citizenship was not for women. One does not have to *strain* to find misogyny in Aristotle; but in Descartes the recognition of the mind or soul as the governing force in humanity is a way of getting beyond gender.

How close is unreconstructed Cartesianism, then, to an innocent Cartesianism about gender? Stanley Clarke has made a good case for the answer 'Very close'.[10] He goes through Descartes's writings, including the scientific writings, and finds textual support not only for a thoroughgoing egalitarianism, which is insufficient for an innocent

---

9 See, e.g., John Passmore, 'Attitudes to Nature' in R. Elliot, ed., *Environmental Ethics* (Oxford: Oxford University Press, 1995), pp. 133ff. See also F. Mathews, *The Ecological Self* (London: Routledge, 1991), pp. 31ff.

10 S. Clarke, 'Descartes's "Gender"' in S. Bordo, ed., *Feminist Interpretations of Rene Descartes* (University Park, Pa.: Pennsylvania State University Press, 1999), pp. 82–102.

Cartesianism about gender in the current signification of 'gender', but also an acknowledgement of gender difference. Clarke argues that Descartes stands out from his philosophical contemporaries in rarely or never using 'valorising' language to downgrade women, and in that his views about sexual generation are markedly untraditional. Not only does Descartes think the materials contributed to reproduction by each sex are on a par – contrary to Aristotle's way of distinguishing between seminal fluid and menstrual discharge – but he is egalitarian in his treatment of love and sexual attraction. It is true, Clarke says, that Descartes's moral ideal – with its emphasis on self-sufficiency and indifference to what is outside one's control – is a recognisably male ideal.[11] It may be true as well that, in his disputes with his intelligent female correspondents about some claims in his moral philosophy, he is unaware of how his own social status as an elite male enables him merely to assert views that require a defence.[12] It is probably true, too, as Clarke admits, that, in general, Descartes's philosophy is without the resources to explain the social ingredients of dominant illusions about what is ideal in men and women. (It is not *wholly* without resources in this area,[13] but they are not always quite what is needed.) Nevertheless, Descartes's philosophy is well able to acknowledge that some of what is thought in advance to be desirable in women can be wholly illusory, just as there can be illusions about what is desirable in human beings generally.

I believe that an innocent Cartesianism about gender has to be built out of innocent Cartesianism about practical reason, and that, as we saw in the previous chapter, this involves departures from Descartes. In particular, Descartes's theory of a sexless soul is an inappropriate vehicle for egalitarianism, because this theory of the soul is objectionable in general. What an innocent Cartesianism needs for an appropriate sensitivity to gender is not the Cartesian soul but a capacity for reflection on one's desires that can incorporate feminist criticism of those desires. The man who would not dream of marrying anyone who was not sexually submissive or fixated on domestic chores has desires that

---

[11] Ibid., p. 98.
[12] Ibid., p. 100. On the other hand, his male correspondents sometimes get the same treatment.
[13] Ibid., p. 99.

are criticisable in the light of feminist arguments, as does the woman who starves herself because she wants to look like a fashion model. Now, the feminist criticism that innocent Cartesianism accommodates is not every kind of feminist criticism. It excludes feminist criticism that dismisses rational criticism itself as a suspect male ideal, for this sort of criticism is self-refuting. But feminist criticism can stop well short of that without making gender undiscussable. A rational reflection that absorbs feminist criticism, then, can be part of innocent Carrtesianism.

Feminist criticism is criticism of a particularly pervasive ideology, and in a sense Cartesianism has always been hospitable to such criticism. We saw (Chapter 2) that Descartes sometimes relies on, and occasionally misuses, the concept of prejudice. Certain mistaken and widespread beliefs about nature are classified as 'prejudices of childhood': These provide some of the material that metaphysical doubt works upon and that natural scientific investigation itself corrects. Apart from the prejudices of childhood, Descartes recognises the prejudices of a certain tradition of teaching. He produces coded criticism of this tradition in the recollections of his schooldays that he includes in the *Discourse*. His correspondence shows that he saw some of the content of traditional teaching in natural science, metaphysics, and moral philosophy as a misguided attempt to bend the theoretical sciences to the requirements of Catholicism. Feminist readings of the theoretical sciences do something similar, only with male power structures replacing those of the Church. Where these readings stop short of including logic and canons of rational criticism among the sciences contaminated by patriarchy, they can be seen as following what is basically a Cartesian strategy.

CARTESIAN SPECIESISM

However innocent Cartesianism turns out to be in relation to women, doesn't its even-handedness stop at the boundaries of the spieces *homo sapiens*? Descartes does not believe that all *natural creatures* are equal, for, as we have already seen in Chapter 4, he thinks linguistic capacity and the adaptability of behaviour set human beings above even the most capable animals. As he says in the *Discourse*, only human behaviour requires the postulation of a mind as its cause – what animals do can be explained with a much more economical conceptual scheme, the same one adequate for explaining the behaviour of automata. The view that animals are automata is not the view that they are simply lumps of matter, or inert artefacts. A thing that has complex internal parts and an organisation that enables it to run on its own is no mean creation. On the other hand, it is not in the same league as human beings. Things with minds have something in common with angels and God; automata are a lower order of thing: They are the artefacts of things with minds.

Some of these views were a source of considerable contention in his lifetime, and Descartes is a major anti-hero in the story told by the animal liberationists about the support for cruelty to animals given by intellectuals.[14] As with claims of misogyny against Descartes, claims that he legitimises callousness towards animals seem one-sided. The textual evidence does not all point in one direction,[15] but it is not impossible to find even in unreconstructed Cartesianism the makings of a biology in which human beings turn out to have a great deal in common with animals. In particular, the idea that in Descartes's theory animals are as incapable of pain as the automated statues that could be seen in seventeenth-century Paris gardens is refutable. After supplying a very abbreviated exposition of Descartes's views in this connection, I shall go on to ask whether this gets Cartesianism off the hook. For even if there is room in Descartes's theory for animal feeling, and so a ground for humaneness, there may be difficulties with what Cartesian rationalism implies is required of us morally in connection with other species and even with certain members of our own. Some of these difficulties confront any rationalist ethics; but others are aggravated by the combination of perfectionism and individualism in an unreconstructed Cartesian ethics.

There are really two theoretical contexts for the views about animals that have been emphasised by Descartes's critics. One context (glimpsed briefly in Chapter 4) is that of the assertion of an ideal of

---

[14] See, e.g., T. Regan, *All That Dwell Therein: Animal Rights and Environmental Ethics* (Berkeley: University of California Press, 1982), ch. 1. See also D. Radner and M. Radner, *Animal Consciousness* (Amherst, N.Y.: Prometheus Books, 1996), p. 64.

[15] I have had the benefit of the excellent survey of this evidence in Enrique Chavez's unpublished Ph.D. thesis, *Descartes on the Substantial Union of Mind and Body*, Reading University, 1994. My exposition, however, runs along rather different lines from his and benefits, in addition, from correspondence with Gabor Boros.

explanatory parsimony in Descartes's early works of natural science. The idea that human beings are uniquely adaptable and linguistically competent is not part of a programme of deifying human beings; rather, Descartes is trying to undo the explanatory profligacy of Aristotelianism. What it took the postulation of several souls to explain in Aristotelian biology, it takes no souls at all to explain in Descartes's. It takes no souls at all to explain the sort of automatic behaviour that deer display when they see a sudden movement or hear a loud noise; that mice display when they see cats; or that human beings display when they sit on a pin. Even if a soul is present in a creature that displays this behaviour, its capacities do not need to be invoked in an explanation of that behaviour. So while a soul *can* be attributed to such a creature, the point of the attribution is not explanatory. Descartes has no objection that I can see to the attribution of a soul to animals as an expression of humane regard[16]; but otherwise, it is gratuitous.

The second theoretical context is ethical. Descartes's theory of practical reason not only directs people to be virtuous but also explains how this is possible for creatures who are sometimes propelled by their unreflective desires and aversions, and who can acquire good and bad habits. Specifically, Descartes considers how a pattern of habitual bodily movement that is bad for an agent can ever be changed, and the answer is that the soul can intervene between stimulus and automatic response. Human beings can in principle change for the better because they can think better of what they have been doing; but creatures with only automatic responses need to be conditioned to change by others who can, so to speak, think better *for* them. The creatures who need such looking after include human children and animals. The relevant distinction is not a species distinction; it is the distinction between automatic behaviour and thought-out or thoughtful behaviour.

To develop the ethical context for Descartes's claims about animality, it is notable that even adult human beings who conform to Descartes's moral ideal, and who can control their behaviour, can have episodes of behaving automatically. Indeed, Descartes suggests

---

[16] It is true that he is alive to, and perhaps worried by, the religious heterodoxy of the idea that animals have immortal souls (cf. his letter to More, 29 November 1646, AT IV 576), but he was alive to the heterodoxy of many theses he asserted.

that soul-involving emotion can give way to automatic emotion in the same person within a relatively short space of time:

[W]hen we hear good news, it is first of all the mind which makes a judgement about it and rejoices with the intellectual joy which occurs without any bodily disturbance and which, for that reason, the Stoics allowed that the man of wisdom could experience.... But later on, when the good news is pictured in the imagination, the spirits flow from the brain to the muscles around the heart and move tiny nerves there, thereby causing a movement in the brain, thereby causing a movement in the brain which produces in the mind a feeling of animal joy. (CSM I, 281; AT VIIIA 317)

Descartes is saying that even in the highest human type – the man of practical wisdom or the Stoic sage – good news can produce a feeling of *animal* joy – that is, the sort of joy that is produced without the intervention of judgement at the time it is experienced. Nor is this described as a lapse or a regrettable falling off from the way joy should be experienced. So long as the joy is at first taken in thinkingly, it can work its subsequent effects unthinkingly.

Now the co-presence of the animal and the rational in human beings is acknowledged elsewhere by Descartes. When human beings look at something absent-mindedly, they take it in just as an animal sees things (CSM III 62; AT I 413–14). It is not as if there is no internal event or as if they are not vaguely aware of what is going on, but it is not at the centre of their attention, and if they react, they do not think out what they do, but carry on so to speak absently. Or so I understand Descartes to be suggesting. Motorway driving is often like this: One goes for miles accommodating the direction and speed of the car to what is registered through vision of other traffic and the curvature of the road. Yet all the time our minds are elsewhere, and if we try to remember the details, we often can't. Descartes, of course, does not go into the phenomenology of absent-mindedness, as I just have, and sometimes the comparison he is making seems to consist of saying that in absent-mindedness some chain of internal events takes place entirely subliminally. This could be said of animals without crediting them with any experience of seeing. If this is what he means, he is badly translated as saying that we see like animals when we see and 'our mind is elsewhere'. Absent-mindedness is a matter of there being a foreground and background to conscious experience; and this is not the distinction between conscious and unconscious. It is clear that Descartes wants *not* to say that animals and humans see in the same way. But in denying it is the same across the species divide he seems intent on denying that in animals to see is to be aware that one sees (CSM III 61–2; AT I 413). And to deny this is not to deny that there is something it is like to see. There is something it is like to see out of the corner of one's eye or absent-mindedly, even if when seeing something out of the corner of one's eye or absent-mindedly, one's focus is elsewhere and not necessarily on seeing.

This unusual and attenuated phenomenology is not much on which to base an attribution to Descartes of a belief in an inner life for animals. But it is *something*. In particular, it is a basis for saying that he does not hold that animals are unconscious or comatose in seeing. On the other hand, he does not believe that absent-minded consciousness is sufficient for self-control. And so he is committed to holding that a human life with a purely animal mentality would be seriously defective.

Though there is room for a kind of animal awareness in Descartes's theory, it is not an awareness that we are *obliged* to postulate, on pain otherwise of leaving animal behaviour unexplained. One could imagine a lot of animal behaviour managed entirely outside the range of consciousness, just as the human body manages digestion or the healing of wounds, or motor reflexes. Because the postulation of an imaginable mechanism adequate to cause a range of observed effects is what Descartes regards as a probable explanation, it is probable for him that animal behaviour is a simple by-product of the circulation of the blood and the operation of the animal spirits within an animal body with a certain organisation of organs. Descartes denies that his probable explanation positively excludes full-fledged thought or reason in animals. As he says in an important letter on this matter to More,

[T]hough I regard it as established that we cannot prove there is any thought in animals, I do not think it can be proved that there is none, since the human mind does not reach into their hearts. But when I investigate what is most probable in this matter, I see no argument for animals having thoughts except this one: since they have eyes, ears, tongues, and other sense-organs like ours, it seems likely that they have sensation like us; and since thought is included in our mode of sensation, similar thought seems to be attributable to them. (CSM III 365; AT V 276–7)

He goes on to rebut this argument, by calling attention to the great range of bodily phenomena that can take place mindlessly in animals. He does not deny that animals, if they are powered by circulating blood and animal spirits, are very sophisticated automata – divinely made ones – incomparably better than those of human manufacture. But he implies that it would be a waste of something as valuable as a soul to be placed in the bodies of things whose behaviour would leave a soul idle.

Significantly, where Descartes *is* content to postulate a soul, namely to explain human conversational and rational agility, he does not positively rule out the possibility that, even there, it might be postulated unnecessarily. A God who can do anything could make a human automaton think, couldn't he? So how can we be sure human beings are not thinking machines? Descartes's answer is that we can't be absolutely sure. We can be morally certain that no physical organs could be disposed to do everything human reason can do (AT VI 57; CSM I 140), but moral certainty falls short of absolute certainty. It is 'for all practical purposes impossible for a machine to have enough different organs' to do everything reason does (AT VI 57; CSM I 140): 'for all practical purposes impossible' is not impossible. This line of thought echoes Descartes's official agnosticism about animal thought.

Even if nonhuman animals are *mere* automata, they are not any old automata – compared with self-moving machines made by humans. They are 'much more splendid' (CSM III 366; AT V 277). This puts even the less sophisticated animals above the automated statues of mythical figures that he admired in Paris parks. Animals, if they are automata, are marvellous automata. Whether, if they are as marvellous as that, we can eat them or kill them with impunity, as Descartes claims later in the letter to More (CSM III 366; ATV 279), is more doubtful. Perhaps they ought to be left alone. This implication is apparently lost on Descartes, at any rate in the letter to More. But even so, it does not seem clear that Descartes is entitled by other things he says to give the vivisectionist or carnivore carte blanche. On his own showing, animals like dogs and horses can be brought to a high state of perfection (CSM III 366; AT V 278). It surely cannot improve them to kill them.

Descartes's doctrine does not always divide animals from humans in the uncompromising way his critics claim, but establishing as much does not make Descartes into a spokesman for animal rights. One has to strain to find passages in which animals are described as highly valuable, and Descartes would have found unintelligible any systematic opposition to the dissection of animals for the acquisition of medical knowledge. On the other hand, as far as I can tell, he does not deny that animals can suffer pain, or that they are capable of complex or sophisticated behaviour. What he denies is that animals are our equals – our equals as intelligent beings or as fellow members of a would-be moral community. Behind these denials is a theory about the limited presence of reason in animals, and the connection between reason and morality.

Isn't the rationalism of Descartes's own theory and of any recognisable Cartesianism likely to undermine it as an approach to morality? Descartes thinks that the only thing, or the principal thing, that merits self-esteem is the virtuous will, and he thinks that the most valuable thing the virtuous will makes possible is self-mastery. This raises the question of the value of the irremediably weak-willed, the value of those who are not yet able to master themselves, and those who are strongly incapable of self-mastery, because they lack the rational capacities of even the weak-willed. Animals fall into the last of these categories, and so do the mentally ill and the mentally incapable among humans. Nothing in Descartes's theory or a Cartesian theory seems to me to imply that these creatures are valueless, or that one can do what one likes with them and to them. On the contrary, the question of what can be done to and with them has to be asked from the standpoint of someone with all his rational faculties, and such a person would presumably see that things that have no capacity for reason can still be damaged, and that there is *prima facie* reason not to damage anything. In other words, nothing in a Cartesian theory seems to me to license or encourage wanton cruelty or vandalism. But this is not to say that a Cartesian moral theory has resources for making sense of respect or esteem for the nonrational. Does it have these resources, and if it does not, is there something seriously wrong with the theory?

Taking first the question of whether it has the resources, I think the answer is both 'Yes' and 'No'. Descartes operates with the concept of a perfection: a property such that, if a thing acquires it, or has it, it lacks nothing. Now an object or person can lack nothing in a dimension of assessment such as beauty or strength, and so merit esteem in that dimension, and yet still be low in the moral pecking order. Someone can be supremely beautiful and weak-willed or supremely strong physically and yet evil. So far great value and great disvalue can co-exist. But in Descartes's framework, or in a rationalist framework recognisable as Cartesian, what one *rationally* does is more properly credited to the agent than how he is endowed by nature or fortune. It is in this spirit that Descartes says that his morally ideal person – the generous person – will not care much about being less good-looking, rich, or intelligent than another person, because attributes like good looks or high intelligence are not in people's control. What really matters, or what matters more than anything else, is moral virtue (CSM I 384; AT IX 447). Descartes does not hold that beauty, intelligence, or riches count for nothing, but that virtue is the only thing for which we ought to give ourselves or other people credit. We are necessarily self-made as virtuous people, but it is possible to be beautiful, rich, or intelligent by birth. To the degree that Descartes can make sense of esteem for perfections independent of the will, it is as assets incidental to a person.

Because there are many inequalities in the natural assets of people, and because some of these inequalities translate into undeserved disadvantage, it is justifiable for there to be a unit of accounting which wipes out that disadvantage by including only what people are responsible for. But the requirements for responsible agency push into prominence species divides, and also the divide, within the class of human agents, between adults and children. If responsibility is the entry condition for being estimable morally, both young children and animals become second-class agents; but if responsibility is eliminated, one denies the strong intuition that natural inequality is compatible with equality as persons. This dilemma faces all moral theorists, not just Cartesian ones; but rationalist theories may face special problems, and Cartesian ones more special problems than others. Rationalist theories tend to regard the direction of moral perfection as running from the natural to the artificial. One starts out with a set of dispositions, and it is by training these or reforming these under the guidance of reason that we improve. In Descartes, and perhaps in the Stoic tradition he draws upon, total self-mastery is the acme of moral reformation. One is never the vehicle for animal impulse unless one willingly and consciously is. We *make* ourselves good by making our actions and inclinations conform to reason. The greater the conformity achieved, the greater degree of moral perfection. Improvement and perfection cannot be achieved except by those who know what their capacities are, and what is possible for human beings in general and for themselves in particular. Nonhuman animals are presumably unable even to make a start on acquiring this knowledge. From the point of view of Cartesian moral theory, then, they are hugely handicapped morally.

There is another, un-Cartesian, way of looking at it: Natural creatures are denatured and harmed when everything they do is thought out or rational or, more generally, the result of training. On this view, rationality is deadening and what matters is life or vitality with no artificial ingredients. From this point of view, the uninhibited beast, including the uninhibited beast in us, is better than the bound and gagged natural spirit that the faculty of reason holds captive inside the Cartesian sage. On this view, the natural is good; and human interference with it, even or perhaps especially in the form of moral discipline, is always a turn for the worse. Death is the worst thing. And ethics is the road to a kind of suicide. I confess that I do not feel in the least attracted by the idea that vitality itself – in the form of aggression or any kind of impulsiveness – is inherently noble. The great gusto with which some people do harmful things – including brawling, killing, and ruthlessly getting rich – does not take away from what is bad or harmful about brawling, killing, and ruthlessly getting rich; on the contrary, it makes it worse. And vitality is certainly consistent with a regime of cruelty to animals and the energetic rape of forests and wilderness.

The fact that there can be moral objections to some of the things arguably done to express the natural spirit within us has put some animal welfarists at odds with some believers in an ecological ethic. There are those who believe that hunting and meat eating are human practices in keeping with the natural order, so long as they are not pursued to the point where they endanger an overall ecological balance. Holders of this view sometimes regard pain as part of animal life and systematic avoidance of pain as something that denatures human beings. On this view – sometimes called the 'land ethic'[17] – welfare can

---

[17] The view is associated with Aldo Leopold. See *A Sand County Almanac* (Oxford: Oxford University Press, 1949). For a more systematic articulation of it as an environmental ethics, see J. B. Callicott, *In Defense of the Land Ethic* (Albany, N.Y.: SUNY Press, 1989).

be at odds with the flourishing of nature in general, and because, again on this view, it is species that count as well as mountains and waters, the death or suffering of individual members of species is not necessarily morally significant. This point of view is deeply un-Cartesian. It devalues medicine, with its fundamental dedication to pain relief, and it devalues the other mechanical arts and sciences, which engineer our domestication, and our estrangement from the wild. Nevertheless, this point of view is sometimes promoted as truer to the standpoint of nature as a whole than welfarism, which favours the conscious and the sentient in the natural world above everything else. In this way the sort of objection that is sometimes made by animal welfarists against those who put human beings above other animals comes back to haunt welfarists themselves. Here, however, welfarists and Cartesians are on the same side. They may not always agree on the distribution of consciousness or on whether animal pain is justified by medical benefit, but at least they agree that conscious creatures are morally more significant than mountains or oceans.

The large question hovering behind the conflict between the land ethic and welfarism, and between the land ethic and Descartes, is whether what it's natural to do can ever be wrong, or, differently, bad for natural creatures. Descartes's answer appears to be 'Yes', and it seems to me to be defensible. But perhaps Descartes's answer is wrong, and in a way that counts against the land ethic as well. Perhaps what it's natural to do is never wrong, and perhaps what it's natural for human beings to do is what it is rational for them to do. I believe that this is roughly the line of thought worked out in Spinoza's metaphysical reaction against Descartes. According to Spinoza, human vitality and human rationality point in the same direction. Far from requiring people to overcome the effects of being embodied minds, ethics gets people to understand and act in keeping with their dependence on God. Human beings are not unions of two substances, according to Spinoza; still less are they distinguished from other things in nature by having both minds and bodies. The mental and physical are pervasive in nature, and there are no substances different from God. Ethics *does* require a discovery of an agency independent of the passions, but this is largely a matter of refusing to be a vehicle for one's conditioned tendencies and contributing actively to one's preservation and improvement. Actively contributing means cultivating the right feelings about one's nature as revealed by philosophy. Philosophy reveals human nature to be open to the influence of the irrational, and to the impersonal forces of a wider nature over which it has little control; but human nature is also expressive of God's properties and God's will, and realising this can be a rational basis for an empowering joy. Empowerment can also come from a political joining of forces with other people. Philosophical self-understanding and politics, then, are important sources for human preservation and improvement. It is in our nature to be able to come to this self-understanding and to engage in politics. Both philosophical understanding and politics are means of self-control, but they are not means of self-control for a reason or self that stands outside nature.

Although Spinoza abolishes some Cartesian dichotomies and has been widely applauded by environmental ethicists for doing so,[18] his system is extremely obscure. For example, it involves concepts of mentality and claims of the pervasiveness of the mental that are at least as hard to understand as the dichotomies in Descartes that they are supposed to overcome. Again, Spinoza's system asserts that in a sense we are passionate by nature and naturally irrational up to a point, though both of these things are to our cost. So nature is a cause of the illness that morality remedies. It follows that nature does not always point us in the same direction as morality, even if something in our nature is the source of morality. In Descartes, there is a natural explanation of some of the obstacles to virtue, but, as nature does not have the exalted status that Spinoza's pantheism gives it, this is not a matter for apologetics. It just turns out that some of the unreflective mechanisms for survival in life are inadequate for a morally flourishing life. Survival is a matter of the continuity of a permanently brittle union of mind and body. Moral flourishing is a sort of fatalistic adjustment of the will on the basis of a deep, partly metaphysical knowledge of one's limitations as an agent. The two kinds of flourishing are of course compatible, but the former does, and the latter does not, depend on things outside the will, and the latter involves undoing some of the pleasure seeking that nature implants to aid mortal survival but that

---

[18] See A. Naess, *Ecology, Community and Lifestyle* (Cambridge: Cambridge University Press, 1989), esp. pp. 84–5. See also F. Mathews, *The Ecological Self,* op.cit. *passim,* and A. Collier, *Being and Worth* (London: Routledge, 1999).

can interfere with virtue. In the end our composite nature explains the tension between the requirements of survival and the requirements of morality. Spinoza banishes that sort of compositeness – the compositeness consisting in a union between two substances. But if Spinoza's metaphysics is supposed to make redundant an explanation of the invitation to immorality in our nature, it conspicuously fails to do so. And its pretensions to present a sort of Cartesianism cleansed of unintelligible dualisms seem to me to go way beyond what is delivered. Obscure syntheses are no better than obscure dualisms.

LESSER PARTS OF WORTHWHILE WHOLES AND RATIONALIST INTERVENTION

There are resources within Descartes for a picture of moral flourishing that does not omit or denigrate animals in particular and the nonhuman natural world in general. The key idea is that of a subject joining itself to other things or recognising itself as a part of other things with which it shares a fate. This approach does not abolish the metaphysical separation between subject and other things, as Spinozistic theories do. On the contrary, only distinct things can be joined. But the approach does allow for worthwhile wholes that individual subjects belong to, and it does suggest senses in which, even if a subject is *metaphysically* complete as a finite mental substance, it can still be better – morally better – to *regard* it as incomplete and act accordingly. This approach points to the possibility of a Cartesianism innocent of anthropocentrism, innocent even of a biocentrism – that is, a bias in favour of the living parts of nature.

The basis in Descartes's writings for what I have in mind is a rarely noticed passage from the letter to Princess Elizabeth of 15 September 1645. He says there that to cultivate a scorn for mere goods of fortune, it helps to think big. It helps in particular to think of the universe as much larger than is supposed by the traditional philosophy. It is better

to have a vast idea of the universe, such as I tried to convey in the third book of my *Principles*. For if we imagine that beyond the heavens there is nothing but imaginary spaces, and that all of the heavens are made only for the service of the earth, and the earth only for man, we will be inclined to think that the earth is our principle abode, and this life our best. Instead of discovering the perfections that are truly within us, we will attribute to other creatures imperfections which they do not possess, so as to raise ourselves above them, and we will be so absurdly presumptuous as to wish to belong to God's council and assist him in the government of the world; and this will bring us countless vain anxieties and troubles. (CSM III 266; AT IV 292)

Not only does the pre-Cartesian philosophy put the Earth at the centre of the universe and man at the centre of terrestrial life; the impression that human beings are the focal point of the universe helps to feed illusions of human preeminence in the government of nature. As emerged in Chapter 1, these illusions are undone by Descartes's physics, which emphasises that much of the history of the cosmos predates human history and that many regions of the universe are entirely removed from human beings and in no way available to be at their service (cf. *Principles*, Part III, § 3CSM I 249; AT VIIIA 81). The passage goes on,

After acknowledging the immensity of the universe, there is yet another truth that is, in my opinion, most useful to know. That is, though each of us is a person distinct from others, whose interests are accordingly in some way different from those of the rest of the world, we ought still to think that none of us could subsist alone and that each one of us is really one of the many parts of the universe, and more particularly a part of the earth, the state, the society and the family. . . . And the interests of the whole, of which each of us is a part, must always be preferred to those of our particular person – with measure, of course, and discretion, because it would be wrong to expose ourselves to a great evil in order to procure only a slight benefit to our kinsfolk or our country. (CSM III 266; AT IV 293)

From the suggestion that we are relatively insignificant parts of the universe Descartes goes on to the idea that our interests as individuals are tied to interests of things bigger and more important than we individually are. Clearly the relevant wider perspective is not just that of society but that conveyed by Part III of the *Principles*, whose frame of reference is nothing smaller than the whole visible universe. This is not an Earth-bound perspective, let alone a merely human perspective, but something altogether broader.

For a subject willingly to join itself to something or someone so as to make a whole with that thing is for a subject to *love* the thing it joins with, in Descartes's technical sense of 'love' (*Passions of the Soul, Pt. 2, §79*; CSM I 356; AT IX 387). *Devotion* is the kind of love in which, when one forms a whole with a thing, one regards oneself as the *lesser* part of the whole. Devotion implies a willingness, if necessary, to die for the preservation of the larger whole (*Passions of the Soul, Pt. 2, §83*; CSM I 358; AT IX 391). So devotion belongs with benevolent love: It goes with wishing the best for the thing with which one forms a whole, as opposed to exulting in the possession of the loved thing. Although the concept of devotion is intended to apply in the first place to a kind of honourable attachment between an individual and his country or family (*Passions of the Soul, Pt. 2, §83*; CSM I 357; AT IX 390), it is clear from the passage just quoted that Descartes is willing to extend the series of family and country to include the Earth and the visible universe. The idea that each human being is and ought to regard himself as a lesser part of the Earth or the universe with which he forms a whole is at least a gesture in the direction of an ecological ethic for which he is routinely supposed to have left no room.

I say that the little apparatus of wholes, parts, and devotion is a step in the direction of an innocent Cartesianism in the area of environmental ethics, but clearly it is *only* a step. Descartes does not comment on the resolutions of conflicts between the requirements of devotion to one's family and the requirements of devotion to one's country, and he is even more elusive in regard to the question of conflicts between devotion to the Earth and devotion to one's country, or devotion to humanity and devotion to Earth. It seems that he is against blind devotion to any larger whole, because he says it takes 'discretion and measure' to decide the extent of sacrifice for the sake of the whole, and the benefit has to be great enough to justify what is done. But it is unclear what factors in a piece of reasoning about self-sacrifice would weigh in a decision to help or not to help the whole. Again, the concept of devotion seems the wrong thing to emphasise in relation to every whole an individual subject fits into. One's state or civil society can command loyalty or affection, but it also requires things – for example, military service or jury service – independently of affection and in virtue of citizenship. This specifically political character of one's relation to one's country is missed by talk of devotion, and nothing else in Descartes's writings fills the gap. Moreover, it would be through the conduct of collective life and not only the conduct of a single life that being part of the Earth and of the universe would be registered by human beings. Here again, however, there is a void in Descartes's writings. On the other hand, the general Cartesian moral injunction to think twice about one's desires and to change them when they are not good for oneself or when they tend to excess suggests that the huge ecological damage due to excessive consumption within a culture of extreme self-indulgence would be heavily condemned by Cartesianism. Indeed, one function of Descartes's missing politics would have been to sketch the kinds of individual self-control required by the public good. It is one thing for a human being to be admonished by a Cartesian morals for harming his health by overeating or by oversatisfying other appetites. It is another thing for the folly of a *social* custom of eating to excess to be registered. The criticism of this sort of custom would belong to a Cartesian politics; so, too, would a criticism of a social custom of overconsumption in areas far outreaching the edible.

It might be thought that this line of reasoning is unavailable to Descartes. When one considers what a recognisably Cartesian politics would say, a first thought is, 'As little as possible'. For it is decidedly Descartes's own conduct that he seeks to regulate by the *morale par provision* of the *Discourse*, not the secular laws and customs regulating the public at large, not the religious rules governing the Catholic faithful. About these he maintains a scrupulous silence. And the range of things one is supposed to have second thoughts about for the sake of morality are always things to do with one's own behaviour. It is as if the criticism of badly grounded beliefs and practices that is licensed by Cartesian rationalism is always supposed to be self-criticism, as if Cartesian rationalism is never primarily a public credo – not officially, anyway. As Descartes writes in Part Two of the *Discourse*,

> . . . I cannot by any means approve of those meddlesome and restless characters who, called neither by birth nor by fortune to the management of public affairs, are yet forever thinking up some new reform. And if I thought that this book contained the slightest ground for suspecting me of such folly, I would be very reluctant to permit its publication. My plan has never gone beyond trying to reform my own thoughts and construct them upon a foundation which is all my own. If I am sufficiently pleased with my work to present you with this sample of it, this does not mean that I would advise anyone to imitate it. (AT VI 14–15; CSM I 118)

Whatever Descartes's intentions were; whatever his circumstances made it imprudent to comment upon, it is hard to see why the injunction never to accept anything as true in the absence of evident grounds stops short of religion or politics or other public matters. And Descartes sometimes got involved in commentary on such matters.

There are two relevant passages in the *Discourse*. The first concerns town planning. Descartes is applying a precept he discovered during his reveries in the stove-heated room, a precept to the effect that the works of a single producer are more satisfying than joint efforts.

> Thus we see that buildings undertaken and completed by a single architect are usually more attractive and better planned than those which several have tried to patch up by adapting old walls built for different purposes. Again, ancient cities which have gradually grown from mere villages into large towns are usually ill-proportioned, compared with those orderly towns which planners lay out as they fancy on level ground. Looking at the buildings of the former individually, you will often find as much art in them, if not more, [as] in those of the latter; but in view of their arrangement – a tall one here, a small one there – and the way they make the streets crooked and irregular, you would say it is chance, rather than the will of men using reason, that placed them so. (AT VI 11–12; CSM I 116)

Here the equation of what is rational with what is better clearly breaks free of the private sphere. And now, to come to my second example, it is the same when Descartes looks back on his own education and distinguishes the learning he valued from the learning he did not. Although this can be represented as an exercise in criticising one's own beliefs and *is* represented that way in the *Discourse* and the *Meditations*, it can equally be interpreted as an attack on a publicly taught curriculum that enshrined the traditional learning and therefore as an attack on the traditional learning itself, not to mention its custodians in the Roman Catholic Church.

RATIONALISM AGAIN

I hope it will be agreed that these applications of Cartesian logic to the public sphere are continuous with applications of rationalism in the West in our own century. One does not have to go back many decades in Western Europe to find exponents of the Cartesian view of town planning actually acting on their distaste for the crooked and irregular and ancient; even the preference for a single planning authority rather than a phalanx of planners is easily recognisable. One can contrast central planning and modernism, which are plausibly said to have a rationalist inspiration, with local, piecemeal activity – typically represented by free-market economic activity; or organically grown cultural activity over time, *alias* tradition, which is not wholly, and perhaps not even primarily, rational. It is clear which side Descartes supports. But how far is this support compatible with the ethic of living as a part of a thing rather than as lord over it? Isn't a policy of *not* intervening obtrusively, and of *not* planning and building from scratch, in better agreement with the status of human beings as minor cogs in the big machine than a policy of intervening aggressively? And isn't Descartes's practical public rationalism at war with such a policy?

The short answer is No. Just as it is necessary for what Descartes regards as a rational decision to give weight to its anticipated bad effects or to the experienced effects of similar decisions in the past, so it is not irrational to reconsider in the light of experience the effects of centralised town planning or fresh starts in other areas of public policy. Perhaps it will be rational, in the light of the record, to conclude that the apparently sensible policy of razing and rebuilding on a grand scale is worse, all things considered, than piecemeal renovation. The idea that there is something in rationalism that makes grand modernising schemes overwhelmingly seductive is itself a kind of illusion. Rationalism is what keeps both theory and practice maximally exposed to criticism. The upshot for the Cartesian science of intervention *par excellence*, mechanics, is instructive. Mechanics or the science of machines is the most concretely world-changing of the sciences in Descartes's scheme: A machine in the narrow sense of the science of mechanics is precisely a device for multiplying the effects of human effort on matter. Mechanics provides apparatus for war, agriculture, building, and transport. But it does not provide guidance as to the use of those products for human benefit. As in medicine, so in mechanics, the requirements of human benefit are worked out from the theory of what it takes to perfect the human body and mind, and by experience of what in fact damages the human body and mind. Clearly certain uses of machines are destructive of these goods, and nothing in Descartes's scheme of the sciences or his rationalism conceals this fact or prevents us from acting in the light of it. There is a corresponding upshot for a would-be green Cartesian politics. It is that the ill effects of human intervention on the nonhuman world can counterbalance whatever counts in favour of intervention. The fact that on Descartes's theory many things in the nonhuman world have the status of automata does not mean that those parts of nonhuman nature cannot suffer ill effects. Automata can be damaged and destroyed. Sometimes their destruction also affects human beings for the worse. In the same way, environmental damage can register as damage in a Cartesian framework. Not only are we supposed to think of ourselves as parts of a bigger natural whole – the Cartesian framework also makes available the thought that we simultaneously depend on and threaten the whole.

Innocent Cartesianism in regard to nonhuman life and inanimate nature does not have to depart very much from original or unreconstructed Cartesianism to get a purchase on green ways of thinking. Or, at least, it does not have to start from entirely new materials. The apparatus of parts and wholes, which is virtually undeveloped in the historical Descartes, is available for the purpose. But it is not the only piece of unreconstructed Cartesianism that promotes ecological thinking. There is also Cartesian natural science, especially its cosmology, which is humbling; and there is Descartes's moral science and his metaphysics. The moral science gives greater value to self-improvement in the form of improvements to the human intellect and the will than to resource-consuming, nature-altering ways of life. The metaphysics gives a reason why the human intellect and the will are the more important and authentic parts of us, and this itself helps to liberate us from appetites ascribable only to us as embodied. Even when we dispense with Descartes's substantial dualism and his version of the soul–body interactionism; even when we work instead with the innocent Cartesian picture of the brain-realised subject, the tendency in Descartes's moral philosophy to asceticism is not undercut. In the face of the ever-increasing and self-damaging demands imposed on nature by human beings, it can make sense to want less of what depends on the Earth and more of what depends only on us. It can make sense even if one does not believe that human beings are essentially immaterial things.

Conclusion

The innocent Cartesianism that emerges from this book is partly a doctrine of human limitation. Human beings are not naturally cut out for natural scientific understanding, and not naturally cut out for an elevated moral and political life. They are not naturally cut out for natural scientific understanding because so little of that is sense-based, and because it is sense-based understandings of things that come naturally to us. To develop sophisticated natural science, human beings have to develop concepts, especially mathematical concepts, that radically revise sense-based understandings. To develop an elevated morals and politics, human beings have to be guided by concepts of individual and collective improvement and not by appetites. The senses and the appetites hold human beings back from the highest degree of human improvement. They are useful for survival, but they also generate much false belief and inevitably unsatisfied desire. The answer to sense-based understanding and appetite alike is reason, or the capacity for standing outside sense-based understanding and appetite and getting beyond them.

In the case of sense-based understanding of the natural causes of appearance, there are two ways of standing outside, according to Descartes. One is the method of doubt; the other is mechanics, or the explanation of appearance by reference to the motions of the parts of bodies. Innocent Cartesianism does not follow unreconstructed Cartesianism in this picture of how to stand outside sensory appearance. First, the success of mathematical physics is well established. No one recognised as a scientist in our own day thinks that a scientific and a sense-based understanding might be one and the same, as Aristotelians did in the early seventeenth century. So a method of doubt that undoes the authority of the senses for the purpose of making acceptable a version of mathematical physics has outlived its usefulness. To the extent that people are able to enter into the current natural scientific conception of the world at all, they must be mathematically trained. The concepts that a mathematical natural science introduces are the main vehicle of detachment from a sense-based understanding that is now recognised to be *wholly* pre-scientific.

In the case of an appetite-based understanding of what we should do in order to flourish, unreconstructed Cartesianism prescribes a single general method of standing outside. One acquires an understanding of the composite nature of human nature, the relative value of the mind and the body in general, and the perfections of which mind and body are capable. One then acts to make oneself more perfect by making one's mind and body more perfect. This is the beginning of moral wisdom. It is not complete wisdom, because one needs to connect the demands of individual improvement with the implications of the dependence of parts on wholes. Individual human beings depend on societies; human beings also depend ontologically on a self-subsistent God, who has made a universe in which human beings are dwarfed by the rest of creation. Acting in the light of these facts is far removed from being propelled by appetites. Human beings need nothing less than metaphysics and physics to inform their practical reasoning.

Innocent Cartesianism departs from unreconstructed Cartesianism about practical reasoning in more than one way. First, it departs from the philosophy of mind of substantial dualism, sticking more closely to the philosophy of mind of mind–body union – that is, the philosophy according to which mind and body are best understood as a working partnership and not as a temporary coincidence of instances of types of substance that essentially have nothing to do with each other. There are things that objectively harm and benefit human beings, but these are not to be gathered only from a theory of what makes mind or body perfect. Again, the picture that Descartes has of mental perfection is too bound up with cognitive and emotional stability – the absence of any reason to revise beliefs and the absence of any reason for regret – to be acceptable to philosophers with no investment in Descartes's picture of God. An innocent Cartesianism about practical reasoning certainly provides for consciousness of the influence of appetites and an ability on the part of agents to reflect on the causes of those appetites and the consequences of satisfying them. It contemplates an elimination or weakening of appetites based on knowledge of those causes and consequences. But it does not take the model of an infallible God who would never revise a decision as something for human life to be guided by. Innocent Cartesianism about practical reasoning frowns on what Frankfurt calls wantons, but it does not make the will into a faculty of inner decision that operates freely only when its objects take into account all natural contingency.

As a doctrine of human limitation, especially human cognitive limitation, innocent Cartesianism has something in common with epistemological scepticism. This is what I was alluding to by saying, in the Introduction, that innocent Cartesianism preserves the realism and respect for scepticism of unreconstructed Cartesianism. It takes seriously the idea that not only our sense-based understanding of the world might fail systematically to identify natural causes, but that even our current non–sense-based concepts might be inadequate. To take these things seriously is to take seriously the lessons of the Dream and Demon hypotheses (Chapter 1). Innocent Cartesianism never declares these hypotheses incoherent, or endorses a programme in epistemology of showing that what human beings think they know, they *do* know for the most part.

In Descartes, the radical doubt of Meditation One is conducted in the first person. The first-person perspective of the doubt might be thought to infect later Meditations in ways that make unreconstructed Cartesianism unacceptable. For example, the first-person perspective of the doubt may exaggerate the importance of consciousness and conscious processes in the mind, when Descartes takes up questions of the nature of the mind. And perhaps that perspective gives consciousness an unwanted prominence in epistemology itself. This latter thought animates criticisms of internalism in epistemology. Many of the processes that lead to the formation of belief are outside consciousness, and many beliefs that are true are not consciously arrived at, still less consciously arrived at by the application of a method. These beliefs would certainly be included among the unexamined and possibly prejudiced beliefs that Descartes thinks have to be sifted through once in a lifetime for a subject to have real *scientia*. How far does innocent Cartesianism preserve the first-person perspective in epistemology and the philosophy of mind?

The answer in both areas is 'To some extent'. Far from saying that everything, or the most important things, about human knowledge or science or the mind are accessible from the first-person perspective, or involve the first-person perspective, innocent Cartesianism insists that *some* things accessible from the first-person perspective or involving the first-person perspective, not necessarily the most important, must be included in a satisfactory analysis of knowledge and in epistemology in general, as well as in a satisfactory philosophy of mind. Some kinds of belief *are* arrived at deliberately and consciously, using conscious principles of belief formation. These are probably untypical of beliefs but require an internalist treatment, one that gives prominence, as unreconstructed Cartesianism does, to the first-person perspective. Other beliefs – innocent Cartesianism allows it to be *most* others – are best handled by an externalist account of knowledge. But even the beliefs that are handled well by externalism do not pre-empt epistemological scepticism, as Chapter 2 shows.

When it comes to the mind, something similar is said by innocent Cartesianism (cf. Chapter 4). Mental states do not *all* have a conscious aspect. But those that do are not open to physicalist reduction. So there is no prospect of a complete physicalist theory of the mind, or even a complete *subpersonal* theory of the mind. This much of innocent Cartesianism is compatible with saying that the brain is the seat of consciousness and the mind. But giving this role to the brain leaves open how consciousness arose in evolutionary history from the brain, and what conceptual domain would be drawn upon by an adequate theory of the mind and the brain. Innocent Cartesianism is compatible with the belief that an adequate such theory is beyond us. But it is also compatible with agnosticism about the accessibility to humans of the theory or the concepts that it requires. In this way innocent Cartesianism, like unreconstructed Cartesianism about mind–body union, makes room for mysterianism as well as for neutral monism.

Unreconstructed Cartesianism about the mind is supposed to suffer from more than its overemphasis on the first person. It is also supposed to overdo the role of reason and to exalt reason unfairly over other human faculties. Here is where empirical criticism of Descartes by Damasio (Chapter 5) links up with criticism of the alleged misogyny of unreconstructed Cartesianism (Chapter 6). As rationalism of a kind is also a staple of innocent Cartesianism, antirationalism may be a significant source of objection to Cartesianism in general. We have already seen that as a doctrine of human limitation and the way human limitation is overcome, innocent Cartesianism is noticeably rationalist. It is the faculty of reason that makes it possible for people to stand outside sense-based conceptions of natural causes. In particular, theoretical reason contributes significantly to an innocent Cartesian success-of-science doctrine (Chapter 3). Reason also makes it possible to stand outside appetite-based policies of action and aspire to something more long term, outward looking, and elevated.

Is even innocent Cartesianism too rationalist? It would be if, as Damasio claims, reason is always supposed to drive out emotion in practical life. It would be if there were no place for the intuitive and the merely traditional in cognitive or practical life. But, as Chapter 6 points out, reason can itself call attention to the disadvantages of subjecting everything – for example, aesthetic judgement – to a requirement of justifiability. There can even be a reason, drawn from the doctrine of human limitation, why, for human beings, too much reason is counterproductive, or why certain requests for reasons can be regarded as hyperrational for human beings that are not hyperrational for every conceivable rational being.

The theory of reason of innocent Cartesianism does not come from science. For one thing it is normative. It does not just call attention to fallings-off from the normal and try to explain them, as in a sense Damasio's theory does. It starts with the normal and points to a way of improving upon that. Scientific reasoning has to strive not only for greater predictive accuracy and explanatory breadth but also for conservation of the successful parts of previously existing successful theories. These desiderata are derived not from science but from philosophical reflection upon it. Practical reasoning has not just got to identify means to ends accepted uncritically but has to be able to produce second thoughts about some ends. In unreconstructed Cartesianism, ends are criticised in the light of an understanding of perfections of body and mind. In innocent Cartesianism, ends are able to be appraised all things considered, including in the light of their consequences for human well-being, and, if this is different, in the light of

Index

absent-mindedness, 152–153
absolute conceptions, 11–12, 42
action(s), xvii–xviii, xix, 139. *See also*
    autonomy; practical reason; will
adaptability, 87, 149
Alston, William, 53–56
angels, 11, 13
animals
    as automata, 150, 154
    linguistic capability and, 87
    senses/appetites in, 4, 127, 140
    speciesism and, x, 138,
      149–160
Anscombe, G. E. M., 24–28
antinaturalism, xvi, 86. *See also*
    naturalism
antirationalism(ists), ix–x, 82, 171. *See*
    also rationalism
antireductionism, 83. *See also*
    mysterianism
anti-scepticism, x, xi, xiii, xiv, 40. *See also*
    scepticism
appetites, xii, 126–128, 130–131, 132,
    166, 167, 168. *See also* emotion(s);
    wantons
Archimedes, 62, 64
Aristotelian sciences, 6–8, 69, 70,
    146–147, 151
Aristotle, 5, 6, 7, 15, 37, 86–87
arithmetic, 7, 9, 15
asceticism, 166
assent, 30, 31
astronomy, 6, 7
atheists, 63
attention, 108

authority, arguments from, xviii, 33–34,
    55–56
automata, 87, 150, 154, 166. *See also*
    machines
autonomy, 33–37, 49, 51, 56, 132, 137
    Cartesian, in common sense, xvii,
    xviii–xix
awareness, 26–27, 28–29. *See also*
    consciousness

Beeckman, Isaac, 33
behaviour. *See* compulsive behaviour;
    ethics/ethical behaviour; impulsive
    behaviour
belief(s)
    common sense and, 49–50
    evidence and, xi, 49–50, 59
    externalism and, 37–44, 53–54,
      170
    false, consciousness of, 4
    formation of, 34, 53–54, 169
    "good reasons" as basis for, xi, 133
    inalienability of, 18–19, 50–51
    indubitability of, xi
    internalism and, 41, 48–52, 169–170
    See also propositions
Blue Book, The (Wittgenstein), 21
body/bodies
    embodiment and, 27, 99, 113, 123
    existence of, 31, 34, 35–37
    heavenly, 6, 37
    movement of, xi
Bordo, Susan, 145–146
Boros, Gabor, 150
brain disorders/injuries, 114–126